Molly's GAME

From Hollywood's Elite to Wall Street's
Billionaire Boys Club, My High-Stakes Adventure
in the World of Underground Poker

Molly Bloom

AN IMPRINT OF HARPERCOLLINS PUBLISHERS

HarperCollins books may be purchased for educational, business, or sales promotional use. For information please e-mail the Special Markets Department at SPsales@harpercollins.com.

FIRST EDITION

Designed by Shannon Plunkett

Library of Congress Cataloging-in-Publication Data has been applied for.

ISBN 978-0-06-221307-5

14   15   16   17   18   OV/RRD   10   9   8   7   6   5   4   3   2   1

This book is dedicated to my mom, Charlene Bloom, who gave me life not once, but twice. Without your fierce love and unwavering support, none of this would have been possible.

CONTENTS

Author's Note

The events and experiences that follow are all true. In some places, I've changed the names, identities, and other specifics of individuals in order to protect their privacy and integrity, and especially to protect their right to tell—or not to tell—their own stories if they so chose. The conversations I re-create come from my clear recollections of them, though they are not written to represent word-for-word transcripts. Instead, I've retold them in a way that evokes the real feeling and meaning of what was said, in keeping with the true essence, mood, and spirit of the exchanges.

Prologue

I am standing in my hallway. It's early morning, maybe five o'clock. I'm wearing a sheer white lace nightgown. High-beam, fluorescent light blinds me.

"PUT YOUR HANDS IN THE AIR," a man's voice yells—he sounds aggressive but emotionless . . . I raise my trembling hands and my eyes slowly adjust to the light.

I am facing a wall of uniformed federal agents stacked back as far as I can see. They are armed with assault weapons—machine guns, guns I have only seen in movies are now pointed at me. "Walk toward us, slowly," the voice commands.

There is a detachment, a lack of humanity in the tone. I realize that they believe I am a threat, the criminal they have been trained to apprehend.

"SLOWER!" the voice warns menacingly. I walk on trembling legs, putting one foot in front of the other. It is the longest walk of my life.

"STAY VERY STILL, NO SUDDEN MOVEMENT," warns another deep voice.

Fear grips my body, making it hard to breathe; the dark hallway begins to look blurry. I am worried I may pass out. I imagine my white negligee covered in blood, and I force myself to stay conscious.

Finally, I reach the front of the line, and I feel someone grab me, and push me roughly up against a concrete wall. I feel hands patting me down, running all along my body; then cold steel handcuffs close tightly around my wrists. "I have a dog, her name is Lucy, please don't hurt her," I plead.

After what feels like an eternity, a female agent yells, "CLEAR!" The man holding me guides me to my couch. Lucy runs over to me and licks my legs.

It kills me to see her so afraid and I try not to cry.

"Sir," I say shakily to the man who handcuffed me. "Can you please tell me what's going on? I think there must be some mistake."

"You are Molly Bloom, aren't you?"

I nod my head.

"Then there is no mistake." He places a piece of paper in front of me. I lean forward, my hands still cuffed tightly behind my back. I can't get past the first line, in black bold letters.

The United States of America v. Molly Bloom

Part One
BEGINNER'S LUCK

Beginner's Luck (noun)

The supposed phenomenon of a poker novice experiencing a disproportionate frequency of success.

Chapter 1

For the first two decades of my life, I lived in Colorado, in a small town called Loveland, forty-six miles north of Denver.

My father was handsome, charismatic, and complicated. He was a practicing psychologist and a professor at Colorado State University. The education of his children was of paramount importance to him. If my brothers and I didn't bring home A's and B's, we were in big trouble. That being said, he always encouraged us to pursue our dreams.

At home he was affectionate, playful, and loving, but when it came to our performance in school and athletics, he demanded excellence. He was filled with a fiery passion that at times was so intense, it was almost terrifying.

Nothing was "recreational" in our family; everything was a lesson in pushing past the limits and being the best we could possibly be. I remember one summer my father woke us up early for a family bike ride. The "ride" ended up involving a grueling vertical climb of three thousand feet at an altitude of almost eleven thousand feet. My youngest brother, Jeremy, must have been six or so, and he rode a bike without gears. I can still see him pedaling his little heart out to keep up, and my dad yelling and screaming like a banshee at him and the rest us to ride faster and push harder, and no complaining allowed. Many years later I asked my dad where his fervor came from. He paused; he had three grown kids who had far surpassed any expectations he could have dreamed of for them. At this point he was older, less fiery, and more introspective.

"It's one of two things," he told me. "In my life and my career, I have seen what the world can do to people, especially girls. I wanted to make sure you kids had the best possible shot." He paused again. "Or, I saw you all as extensions of myself."

From the other direction, my mother taught us compassion. She believed in being kind to every living thing and she led by example. My beautiful mother is the most gentle and loving person I have ever known. She is smart and competent, and instead of pushing us to conquer and win, she encouraged us to dream, and took it upon herself to nurture and facilitate those dreams. When I was very young, I loved costumes, so naturally Halloween was my favorite holiday. I would wait anxiously each year, laboring over who or what I would be that year. My fifth Halloween I couldn't choose between a duck and a fairy. I told my mother I wanted to be a duck-fairy. My mother kept a straight face.

"Well then, duck-fairy you shall be." She stayed up all night constructing the costume. I, of course, looked ridiculous but her nonjudgmental support of individuality inspired my brothers and me to live outside the box and forge our own paths. She fixed the cars, mowed the lawn, invented educational games, created treasure hunts, was on every PTA board, and still made sure she looked beautiful and had a drink in hand for my father when he got home from work.

My parents parented according to their strengths: my brothers and I were guided by their combined feminine and masculine energies. Their polarity molded us.

MY FAMILY WENT SKIING EVERY WEEKEND during my childhood. We would pile into the Wagoner and drive two hours to our one-bedroom condo in Keystone. No matter what the conditions were—blizzards, stomachaches, sixty below zero, we were always the first ones on the mountain. Jordan and I were talented, but my brother Jeremy was a prodigy. We all soon caught the attention of the head coach of the local mogul team and we began training and soon even competing.

During the summers, we spent our days water skiing, biking, running, hiking. My brothers played Pee Wee football, baseball, and basketball. I started competing in gymnastics and running 5K races. We were always moving, always training to go faster, be stronger, push harder. We didn't resent any of it. It was what we knew.

At twelve, I was running a 5K when I felt a white-hot pain between my shoulder blades. After a unanimous first, second, and third opinion, I was scheduled for emergency spinal surgery. I had a rapid onset of scoliosis. My parents waited nervously during my seven-hour surgery while the doctors cut me open from neck to tailbone and carefully straightened my spine (which looked like an S and was curved at sixty-three degrees) by extracting bone from my hip, fusing the eleven curved vertebrae together, and fastening metal rods to the fused segment. Afterward, my doctor gently but firmly informed me that my competitive sports career was over. He droned on, telling me all the activities I could not do and how one can lead a very fulfilling and normal life, but I had stopped listening.

Quitting skiing was simply not an option. It was woven too tightly into the fabric of my family. I spent a year recovering. I was homeschooled and I had to spend most of the day in bed. I watched longingly as my family left every weekend without me, sitting in bed while they flew down the slopes or went out on the lake. I felt ashamed of my brace and my physical limitations. I felt like an outsider. I became even more determined to not let my surgery affect my life. I longed to feel a part of my family again; to feel the pride and hear the praise of my father, instead of the pity. With each lonely day I grew more and more determined to never again sit life out. As soon as the X-rays showed that my vertebrae had successfully fused, I was back on the mountain, skiing with a fierce determination, and by midseason I was winning in my age division. By then, my younger brother Jeremy had taken the freestyle skiing world by storm. He was ten years old and already dominating the sport. He was also exceptional in track and football. His coaches told my father they had never seen anyone as talented as Jeremy. He was our golden boy.

My brother Jordan was also a talented athlete, but his mind was his greatest attribute. He loved to learn. He loved to take things apart and figure out how to put them back together. He didn't want to hear imaginary bedtime stories; he wanted to hear stories about real people in history.

My mom had a new story every night for him, about great world leaders or visionary scientists, and she researched the facts and wove them into engaging tales.

From a very young age, Jordan knew he wanted to be a surgeon. I remember his favorite stuffed animal, Sir Dog. Sir Dog was Jordan's first patient and underwent so many procedures he began to look like Frankenstein. My dad was delighted with his brilliant son and his ambition.

My brothers' talents and ambitions presented early and I watched those gifts earn them the accolades that I desperately wanted. I loved to read and write, and when I was young I lived half my life in books, movies, and my imagination. In elementary school I didn't want to play with other kids; I was shy and sensitive and I found them intimidating. So my mom spoke to the school librarian. Tina Sekavic agreed to allow me to hang out in the library, so I spent the next few years reading biographies about women who had changed the world like Cleopatra, Joan of Arc, Queen Elizabeth, and others. (My mom had initially suggested this, but I quickly became fascinated.) I was moved by their bravery and determination, and I decided right then and there, I didn't want to settle for an ordinary life. I craved adventure; I wanted to leave my mark.

When my brothers and I reached our teenage years, Jordan's academic prowess continued to surpass his peers. He was two years younger than I was when he tested out of his grade's science and math classes and was placed in mine. Jeremy broke records in track, led the football team to the state championship, and was a local hero. My grades were high, and I was a good, sometimes great, athlete. But still, I hadn't unearthed any talent as impressive as those of my brothers. The feelings of inadequacy increased and drove me almost obsessively to somehow prove my worth.

As we got older, I watched my father invest himself more and more in my brothers' goals and dreams. I became tired of always being on the outside, I wanted the attention and approval too. The issue was that I was a dreamer, and inspired by the heroines in my books. I had grand ambitions that fell far outside my father's pragmatism. But I still desperately craved his approval.

"Jeremy is going to be an Olympian, and Jordan will be a doctor. What should I be, Dad?" I asked him on an early morning chairlift.

"Well, you like to read and argue," he started, which felt like a thorny compliment. In fairness, I was that annoying teenager who questioned every opinion or decision my parents made.

"You should be an attorney."

And so it was decreed.

I went off to college, I studied political science, and I continued to compete in skiing. I pledged a sorority, in an effort to be well rounded, but when the organization's mandatory social requirements got in the way of my real goals, I quit. I had to work hard for my grades, and even harder to overcome my physical limitations in skiing. I was obsessed with success, I was driven by an innate ambition, but more than that by a need for praise and recognition

The year I made the U.S. national ski team, my dad had a sit-down with me.

"Shouldn't you focus on school, Molly? I mean how far are you going to go with this thing? You have far exceeded any expectations anyone had of you." Though they never said it, everyone had pretty much stopped taking my skiing career seriously after my back surgery.

I was devastated. Instead of the visions I had of my father looking at me with the same proud smile he gave Jeremy the year before when he had made the national team, he was trying to talk me out of it.

The hurt only further fueled my determination. If no one else would believe in me, I would believe in myself.

That year Jeremy finished third overall in the country, and to the shock of my family, so did I. I remember standing tall on the podium, a medal around my neck and my long hair in a ponytail.

I got home that night and ignored the pain in my back and neck. I was tired of living with pain and pretending it wasn't there. I was exhausted from trying to keep up with my superstar brother and I was especially tired of feeling like I had to constantly prove myself. Still, I had made the U.S. Ski Team and I had placed third overall. I felt satisfied. It was time to move on—on my own terms now.

I RETIRED FROM SKIING. I didn't really want to be around for the fallout from that decision, though I suspected that despite my third-place finish, my father would still be relieved. To get away, I signed up for a study abroad in Greece. I instantly fell in love with the unfamiliarity and uncertainty involved in being in a foreign place. Everything was a discovery, a riddle to solve. Suddenly my world became a lot bigger than seeking my father's approval. Somewhere, someone else was winning a blue ribbon in women's moguls, or acing an exam, but frankly I didn't care. I was especially enamored with the Gypsies in Greece. When I think about them now, they weren't so unlike gamblers—seeking out angles, adventure, ignoring rules, and living an unfettered, free life. I made friends with some Gypsy kids in Crete. Their parents had been rounded up and shipped back to Serbia, so they were on their own. The Greeks are very wary of foreigners, understandable for a nation that has had a long history of occupation. I bought these kids food, and medicine for their baby. I spoke conversational Greek, and their Gypsy dialect was similar enough that we were able to communicate. The leader of the Gypsies' tribe heard about what I had done for the children and invited me to their camp. That was an amazing experience. I decided to do my honors thesis on the legal treatment of nomadic people. It saddened me that these people couldn't travel freely, as they had done for hundreds of years, and it seemed they had no advocates or representation. Their way of life was entirely free. It was so different from the life I had known. They loved music, food, dancing, falling in love, and when a place became stale they went somewhere else. This particular tribe was opposed to stealing, and instead focused on art and commerce to make their living.

I spent an extra three months after my program ended traveling by myself, staying in hostels, meeting interesting people, and exploring new places. I returned to the States a different girl. I still cared about school, but now I cared just as much about life experience and adventure. And then I met Chad.

Chad was good-looking, fast-talking, and brilliant. He was a deal maker and a hustler. He taught me about wine, took me to expensive restaurants, took me to my first opera, gave me amazing books to read.

Chad is the one who took me to California for the first time. I'll never forget the drive along the Pacific Coast Highway. I couldn't believe this place was real. We went to Rodeo Drive, had lunch at the Beverly Hills Hotel. Time seemed to slow down, as if Los Angeles was one never-ending perfect day. I watched the beautiful people—they all seemed so content and happy.

Los Angeles felt almost dreamlike and not governed by reality. I had started to rethink my plan to live in Greece, and Los Angeles solidified my thoughts; I wanted to take a year off to be free, no plan, no structure, and just live. I had chased winter (even during the summers my brother and I would attend ski camp on the glaciers in British Columbia) and the dreams of what I thought my father had in store for me for as long as I could remember. I was filled with excitement at the idea of an uncharted path. Law school could wait, it was just a year.

Chad tried everything to get me to stay in Colorado, including buying me an adorable beagle puppy. But my mind was made up. I appreciated what Chad had given me—which were the tools to create a new life—but I didn't love him.

He let me keep the dog. I named her Lucy. She was so badly behaved that she got kicked out of every puppy day care and obedience class I took her to. But she was sweet and smart and she loved and needed me. It was nice to be needed.

No matter how much I tried to explain my decision, my parents refused to fund my undefined California hiatus. I had saved about $2,000 from a babysitting job I had taken over the summer. I had one friend in L.A. named Steve, who had been on the ski team with me. He had reluctantly agreed to a limited stay on his couch.

"You need to have a plan," he lectured me over the phone one day while I was driving on the highway to Los Angeles. "L.A. isn't like Colorado, nobody will notice you here," he said, trying to prepare me for the harsh reality of this place. But when I put my mind to something, nothing and nobody can dissuade me; it's been a strength and, at times, a huge detriment.

"Mmm-hmm," I said, staring at the desert horizon, halfway to my next adventure.

Lucy sat copilot, sleeping.

"What is your plan? Do you even have one?" Steve asked.

"Of course, I'll get a job and get off your couch, and then I'll take over the world," I joked.

He sighed. "Drive safely," he said. Steve always had been risk-averse.

I hung up the phone and fixed my eyes on the road ahead.

 13

IT WAS NEARLY MIDNIGHT when the 405 started descending into Los Angeles. There were so many lights, and each light had a story. It was so unlike the stretches of darkness in Colorado. In L.A., the light far outweighed the dark—the lights represented a whole world waiting to be discovered. Steve had made up the couch for Lucy and me and we crashed hard after our seventeen-hour drive. I woke up early, and the sun was streaming through the windows. I took Lucy outside for a walk. L.A. smelled heavenly, like sunshine and flowers. But if I wanted to stay, I needed to get a job STAT. I had a little waitressing experience and I felt like that was my best bet since you could make tips right away as opposed to waiting for a weekly paycheck. Steve was up when I returned.

"Welcome to L.A.," he said.

"Thanks, Steve. Where do you think is the best place for me to get a waitressing job?"

"Beverly Hills would be the best, but it's really hard. Every pretty girl is an out-of-work actress or model and they are all waitresses, it's not like—"

"I know, Steve, I know it's not Colorado." I smiled. "How do I get to Beverly Hills?"

He gave me directions and wished me luck with doubtful eyes.

He was right, most places I tried were not hiring. I was greeted icily by one pretty hostess after another who gave me a disdainful once-over and explained haughtily that they were fully staffed and I could fill out an application but it would be a waste of time because there were so many other applicants.

I was starting to lose hope as I walked into a last restaurant on the street.

"Hi! Are you hiring?" I asked with my biggest, brightest, most hopeful smile.

Instead of being a slender, perfectly put-together mean girl, the person in front of me was a man in his 'forties. "Are you an actress?" he asked suspiciously.

"No."

"Model?"

"No." I laughed. I was five four on my tallest day.

"Is there any reason you would ever have to go to a casting?"

"Sir, I don't even know what that means."

His face relaxed.

"I have a breakfast shift. You need to be here at five A.M., and when I say five A.M., I mean four forty-five A.M."

I smiled bigger to conceal my horror at this ungodly hour.

"No problem," I said firmly.

"You're hired," he said, then explained to me about the uniform, which was a pressed, heavily starched, white dress shirt, a tie, and black pants. "Don't be late, I don't tolerate tardiness." he said, and walked away quickly to berate some poor employee.

IT WAS STILL DARK when I drove to the restaurant. I had borrowed an oversized shirt and tie from Steve. I looked like a puffy penguin.

My new boss, Ed, was already inside, along with another waitress. There was only one customer. He led me through the restaurant explaining my duties and informing me proudly that he had worked there for fifteen years, and he basically, as far as I was concerned, owned the place. He was the only one who had the ear of the owner, who was very rich and very important, and if I saw him I was never to address him unless Ed had instructed me to do so. The owner had many rich, important friends, known as VIP's, and we were to treat them all like God.

After my training session, Ed dispatched me to serve.

"VIP," Ed mouthed dramatically.

I gave him a thumbs-up, trying to hide my contempt.

The customer was a cute little old man.

I walked up with a megawatt smile. "Hi there! How is your morning so far?"

He looked up, his pale watery eyes squinting at me. "Aren't you something. Are you new?"

I smiled. "I am. It's my first day."

He nodded. "Thought so, turn around," he demanded, tracing a circle in the air with bony fingers.

I turned around, and looked at the front of the restaurant, trying to see what he wanted me to see. There was nothing of note.

I looked back at him, confused.

He was nodding in approval.

"I'd like you to be my special friend," he said. "I'll pay your bills and you can help me out." He winked.

Now I was utterly confused, and my face must have shown it.

"I'm a diabetic," he began. "So I can't even get it up," he continued, reassuring me. "I just want affection and attention."

My expression went from confused to aghast. Oh my God, this old man who could've have been my grandfather was propositioning me. I was mortified. I felt the blood rush to my face. I wanted to tell him off, but I had been taught to always respect my elders. I wasn't sure how to handle this. I had to find Ed.

I mumbled something and rushed off.

I approached Ed, my face burning.

"Ed, I know he's a VIP but he . . ." and I whispered the proposal into Ed's ear.

Ed looked at me blankly

"So what's the problem? I thought I discussed the policy on VIP's."

I looked at him incredulously. "Are you serious? I'm definitely NOT going back over there. Can someone else take the table?" I asked.

"Molly, it's not even two hours into your shift and you're already causing problems. You should count yourself lucky that one of the VIP's has taken a liking to you."

I felt my chest fill with hot anger.

Ed looked at me with a sneer. "That offer might be the best you will ever have in this town."

I rushed out of that restaurant as fast as I could, but the tears were coming hard and fast. I ducked into an alley and tried to pull myself together.

STILL WEARING MY UNIFORM, I walked toward my car.

A shiny silver Mercedes sped by at an alarming speed and pulled onto the sidewalk in front of me, nearly obliterating me.

Perfect. Could this day get any worse? A young, good-looking guy wearing army fatigues and a rhinestone-skull T-shirt exited the coupe, slamming the door and shouting at his cell phone.

He stopped screaming as I passed him.

 16

"Hey, are you a waitress?"

I looked down at my uniform.

"No. Yes. Well, I mean, I . . ." I stumbled for words.

"You either are or you're not, it's not a hard question," he demanded impatiently

"Okay, yes," I said.

"Stay there," he ordered.

"ANDREW!" he yelled.

A man in a chef's coat walked out of a restaurant and approached us.

"Look, I found you your waitress, so stop crying. FUCK! Do I have to do everything around here?"

"Does she have experience?"

"How the fuck should I know?" the man barked.

Andrew sighed and said, "Come with me."

We walked inside a restaurant, which was filled with frenetic energy: the construction workers—drilling, pounding, polishing; the designer in midtizzy because he ordered powder-pink peonies, and not soft pink, bartenders stocking the bar, and the waiters doing side work. "Our soft opening is tonight," said Andrew. "We're short-staffed and construction isn't even finished." He wasn't complaining. He was just worn down.

I followed him into a beautiful vine-covered courtyard, an oasis amid the chaos. We sat on a wooden bench, and he began to grill me.

"How do you know Reardon?" he asked.

I assumed that Reardon was the terrifying man with the silver Mercedes.

"Um, he almost hit me with his car," I answered,

Andrew laughed appreciatively. "Sounds about right,"

"How long have you been in L.A.?" he asked kindly

"About thirty-six hours," "I said.

"From where?"

"Colorado."

"Something tells me you don't have fine dining experience."

"My mom taught the manners class at my school, and I'm a fast learner," I offered.

He laughed.

"Okay, Colorado, I have a feeling I'm going to regret it, but we will give you a shot."

"What's your policy on VIP's?" I asked.

"It's Beverly Hills. Everyone is a fucking VIP," he said.

"So hypothetically, if a gross, perverted old man tries to solicit you, do you have to wait on them?"

"I'll throw them out on their old ass,"

I smiled. "When do I start?"

Chapter 2

*F*rom the outside, Boulevard, the restaurant where I'd just
been hired, looked dark and mysterious. When I walked
in, I saw the young Hollywood set lounging on suede ottomans and leather
banquettes. I felt as if I were crashing a private party.

I arrived thinking it would be like the other jobs I'd had. I would
receive some training and then start, but that wasn't the kind of place
Reardon Green ran: it was sink or swim in his world. Everyone was rushing around, nobody had a second to answer a question, and I was constantly in the way. I stood in the middle of the whirlwind and took a
deep breath. It appeared I didn't have any tables assigned to me yet, so
I started doing laps around the restaurant clearing plates and refilling
drinks. I placed a lemon-drop martini in front of a woman I recognized
from some show on television.

"Oh, actually, can you bring me the whole lemon?" she asked me.

She turned to her fellow diners. "I like to cut it myself—just to make
sure it's really fresh. You see them sitting out there in those plastic bins
covered with flies." She shuddered and the whole table shuddered with
her. Of course, then they all wanted to garnish their own drinks now. I was
sent off to find an orange, a lemon, and a lime.

The walk to the kitchen took me past tables full of celebrities and socialites, and I tried not to stare at the A-list faces I had seen in magazines but never in person. As I pushed through the kitchen doors, the noise of the dining room receded behind me.

The kitchen had its own sound, a symphony of orders and acquiescences, the clink of plates, the thud of heavy iron pots, and the hiss of meat hitting a pan. Andrew was screaming at the sous-chefs and hurrying plates to go out to the tables. I rushed through it all and made for the fridge, trying not to bother anyone or get in the way. In my hurry, I turned the wrong way and found myself in a supply closet where Cam, one of the owners, was leaning back against a mountain of paper towels with his pants around his ankles. I stopped dead in my tracks. This was by far the most humiliating moment of my life.

"Sorry!" I whispered, still frozen in my tracks.

He smiled at me, affable and completely unembarrassed.

"What's up!" he said. "Wanna be in my movie?"

He pointed toward the security camera on the ceiling and widened his boyish grin, raising his hand for me to high-five him. The girl who squatted on her knees in front of him giggled. I did not want to insult him, so I gingerly leaned over the girl and quickly slapped his palm. Then I fled as fast as I could, my face burning with embarrassment.

What had I signed on for?

A WEEK AFTER I STARTED WORKING at the restaurant, I went to a party with Steve. I was standing and listening to everybody talk about the pilots they were shooting and the scripts they were writing, feeling very much like an outsider, when a pretty girl grabbed my hand.

"Who cares?" she whispered in my ear. "Let's take a shot!"

She was dressed head to toe in designer clothes, carrying a bag that was worth more than my car. I followed her into the kitchen. Three tequila shots later, she was my new best friend.

Blair was a party girl, but she was down-to-earth and kind, and she seemed not to have a care in the world. She was the heir to a peanut butter fortune, and her family had houses all over the world, including Beverly Hills, where she had spent her childhood before being shipped off to a fancy private school in New York.

A couple of young girls walked into the kitchen, and Blair flinched. I recognized one of the girls from a popular MTV reality show.

"Oh shit!" Blair said, grabbing the tequila bottle with one hand and my arm with the other. She dragged me into a bathroom down the hallway.

"I hooked up with that girl's boyfriend and she caught us. She wants to kill me!"

I started laughing as she tipped the bottle back and took a swig. We spent most of the night in the massive marble bathroom, laughing and taking shots, talking about our lives and our big plans for the future. I told her about my living situation—because in a week I wouldn't have one. Steve had laid down the law.

"Oh my God! Move in with me!" she squealed. "My apartment is gorgeous, you will love it. I totally have an extra room."

In one drunken night, hiding in a bathroom from a scorned reality star, I found a new comrade and a place to live.

That was L.A. You just never knew what would happen when you left the house.

I DIDN'T LOVE WAITING TABLES, and to be honest, I was pretty terrible at it, but the restaurant was a way into this strange new world, composed of three primary layers: the staff, the customers, and my bosses.

The staff was not your normal restaurant employees. They were all aspiring musicians, models, or actresses and most of them were actually very talented. The waiters were usually aspiring actors who treated their restaurant position simply as a role they were playing. I observed them as they got into character, put their ego aside, and became who they needed to be for the table: flirt, the frat boy, the confidant. The bartenders were usually musicians or models. The girls were sexy and glamorous, and they knew how to work a room. I studied their ability to be flirtatious and coy at the same time. I practiced doing my hair and makeup the way they did, and I took note of the sexy outfits they put together. I tried to make myself small, and take it all in.

The customers were larger than life: celebrities, rock stars, CEO's, finance wizards, actual princes; you never knew who would show up. Most of them had a pretty healthy sense of entitlement, and keeping them happy all the time was next to impossible. I learned little tricks, though, like speaking to the women first and primarily (for the date tables) or being efficient but invisible during business lunches. I was good at reading human behavior but terrible at food service. I was constantly dropping plates, forgetting to clear certain forks, and I was a disaster at opening wine in the ceremonious way the owners required.

But to me, the most interesting characters of all were Reardon and his two partners.

Reardon was brilliant, impatient, volatile, and impossible. He was the brains of the operation.

Cam was the son of one of the richest men in the world. His monthly trust-fund checks were enough to buy a small island. He seemed to take little interest in the business and, as far as I could tell, spent his time womanizing, partying, gambling, and indulging in every hedonistic vice you could imagine. He was the money; his role was signing off as the guarantor.

Sam had grown up with Cam. He had brilliant people skills. He was charming, hilarious, and he knew how to schmooze better than anybody I had ever seen. I guess he was the head of marketing and client relations.

Watching the three of them interact was like observing a new species. They did not live in the same world I had known for the last twenty-some years. They were over the top, unfazed by consequence and had a total disregard for rules and structure.

THE FORMULA AT THE RESTAURANT was the same as at any in Beverly Hills that hoped to survive—provide the discerning customer with the best of everything. The partners had spent a small fortune on Frette linens, Riedel glassware, and wines from the finest vineyards. The servers were attractive and professional, the chef was world-renowned, and the decor was beautiful.

The inviting atmosphere that the staff created was part of our act. Our politeness was the curtain that concealed the frenzy that was always threatening to surface. You see, the bosses expected perfection and professionalism—that is, until they got a couple drinks in them and would easily forget their carefully laid plans.

One Sunday morning, I went to open the restaurant for brunch, and discovered that Sam, a DJ, and a bunch of girls were still there partying. Sam had turned our fine dining restaurant into his very own seedy after-hours club. I tried explaining to him that I needed to open the large suede curtains and remove the makeshift DJ booth so that I could ready the restaurant for service. He replied in gibberish.

"Dumb, dumb, dumb, dumb . . ." he garbled, and closed the curtains as quickly as I opened them.

I called Reardon. "Sam is still here partying. He won't leave and he won't let me open the restaurant, what should I do?"

"Goddammit! Fuck! Put Sam on the phone. I'm coming down there."

I handed Sam the phone.

"Dumb dumb dumb dumb," he continued to Reardon, and handed me back the phone.

"Get him in a cab!!" yelled Reardon.

I looked around the room, but Sam had disappeared.

"Wait, I think he's gone," I said.

Just then, I looked out the window. Sam, with his large-face gold Rolex, polished Prada shoes, and beige silk pants, was outside boarding a bus. I ran out to try to stop him. I started laughing into the phone.

"What's going on, what's he doing?" Reardon demanded.

"He's getting on the bus to downtown L.A."

"As in public transportation?"

"Yep," I replied as a happy and obliterated Sam waved cheerfully to me from his seat on the bus.

"Jesus." Reardon sighed. "Tell the Hammer to pick him up."

The Hammer was the guys' security slash limo driver slash money collector. I heard he had recently gotten out of jail for something, but no one would tell me what.

I called the Hammer, who grumpily agreed to take the "sled," which was what Sam had named the company limo, to find Sam somewhere in the streets of downtown. When I hung up and turned around, the DJ and the girls were just about to open a thousand-dollar bottle of Louis XIII champagne.

I swooped in and grabbed the bottle.

"No, no, no! Time to go home, guys," I said. I turned off the music like a parent busting up a party and ushered them out onto the street.

I managed to get the restaurant open in time for brunch and the Hammer eventually found Sam walking the streets of Compton with a bottle of Cristal champagne and some interesting friends. It seemed like every day at the restaurant was more absurd than the last, but it wasn't ever boring.

Chapter 3

*Y*ou're the worst fucking waitress we've ever seen," Reardon barked to me after a shift one day. I was aware of the limitations of my aptitude for servitude, but the worst ever? Really? My stomach plunged . . . Was I getting fired?

"The worst," he repeated. "But there's something about you. Everybody likes you. People come back just to talk to you."

"Thanks?" I said tentatively.

"Why don't you come work for us?"

I looked at him in confusion.

"For our real-estate development fund. We just raised two hundred and fifty million dollars."

"What would I do?" I asked, treading carefully.

"Don't ask stupid questions. What do you care? It's better than serving food and you'll learn a lot."

I snorted under my breath, thinking of all the ridiculous shenanigans I had seen in the last couple months.

"Oh, you think you're smart? You're not fucking smart. You don't know anything about the way the world works."

It wasn't a very gracious job offer, but I wasn't getting fired either.

So I said, "Okay, I'll do it."

"No shit," replied Reardon.

WORKING AT THE REAL-ESTATE FUND eliminated the other layers from my life and it was all Reardon, Sam, and Cam, all the time. They were like their own fraternity. They had their own rules, they even had their own language. It goes without saying that they were from a completely different world than I was. What seemed like once-in-a-lifetime opportunities to me—Sundance, Oscar parties, yacht trips—were their casual weekend plans. Their friends were celebrities, famous athletes, billionaires, and socialites. I began to spend my days and nights doing various tasks for them, always watching from the sidelines, secretly hoping to be invited into their club.

Reardon would come into my office at 8:30 P.M. on a Friday and say, "Get me a reservation for nine tonight at [insert the name of the hottest, most impossible restaurant to get a reservation at here]."

I would call and the hostess would laugh and hang up.

"They're fully booked," I would tell him.

He would then erupt in a fury: "You're the biggest fucking idiot I've ever met. What's wrong with you? How do you expect to get anywhere in life if you can't even get a reservation at some stupid fucking restaurant."

He made me so nervous that I would start garbling my words or tugging on my hair.

"Speak! Speak! Don't touch your face. Don't fumble around!" he would demand.

That was the scenario for my early learning curve; every day felt like I was on the front lines of battle.

One morning he called at five thirty, waking me up.

"Need you in the office, now," he ordered. "Pick up bagels." He hung up. Reardon never said hello or good-bye. He was a straight-to-the-point kind of guy.

I groaned and dragged myself into the shower.

I barely had time to dry off before I received a follow-up text message.

Where the fuck are you?

I drove as fast as I could to the office hoping to pass a bagel shop. The only thing I saw was the Pink Dot grocery. I ran in and grabbed some bagels and cream cheese. My hair was wet and my eyes were barely open, but I made it to the office, with breakfast, in record time.

"Where are my bagels?" said Reardon, in lieu of "good morning."

I placed the bag on his desk.

He ripped open the bag. Reardon never just opened things, he annihilated everything in his path.

"WHAT THE FUCK IS THIS?" he yelled.

I jumped. By now I should have been used to the sudden fury that Reardon could unleash, but it still took me by surprise sometimes.

"Are these from PINK DOT?" Apparently Pink Dot was a low-rent, late-night kind of grocery store.

"You might as well have stopped at a FUCKING homeless shelter!" he screamed. "I DO NOT EAT FUCKING BAGELS FROM FUCKING PINK DOT. THESE ARE FUCKING POOR PEOPLE BAGELS." He hurled the bag at me. I ducked just in time.

"Where would you like me to get your bagels in the future?" I asked in a deliberately calm voice, hoping my adultlike tone would allow him to see he was behaving like a temperamental two-year-old.

"Go get the car," he barked.

I chauffeured him to Greenblatt's to pick up bagels for real "players."

He had me drop him off at his meeting.

"Wait here," he said.

"For how long?" I asked.

"Until I come back, stupid." He laughed, slamming the door.

EVENTUALLY REARDON STARTED BRINGING ME to the meetings instead of making me wait outside. I observed him closely. Reardon was a master negotiator. He was able to convince really smart people to make really stupid decisions. He would walk into a meeting, and by the time he walked out, he was carrying signed agreements that met all of his insane demands: he would assume none of the risk and had the final say in all decisions. It didn't matter who his opponent was, he outplayed them every time. I came to recognize the checkmate moment in which the Ivy League guy with his custom suit and air of arrogance would suddenly realize the guy wearing army fatigues and a skull T-shirt, who had partied his way through a state university, had just crushed him. I had to hide my smile as Mr. Pedigree's elitist expression deflated into withering defeat.

There was no university on the planet that could have prepared me for the education I got from Reardon. It was baptism by fire. It was frustrating, and it was challenging, but I loved every class. I loved the show. I loved watching him succeed. In order to survive in his world, I had to learn how to operate well under pressure, and so he tightened the screws in order to teach me. Reardon was like a more extreme version of my father, always pushing me, never allowing me to take it easy, wanting to make me tough. He gave me a Wall Street–style education, the kind that guys give guys down on the floor or at the trading desk, the kind that women rarely get. I started to see the world for what it was, or at least his world. I also saw that there were more than just the traditional, safe routes to success.

Reardon became my grad school and I studied how he operated. Law school wasn't even on my radar anymore. Reardon was a master strategist. He knew how to analyze a deal, and if he recognized opportunity, he would capitalize on it. It didn't matter if it was something he had no experience in, he would learn. Study it day and night, until he figured it out.

The lessons I got from Reardon on how to actually conduct business were, however, ludicrously short on detail.

"We're going to Monaco, Molly. Take care of the company."

They'd go party for four weeks; all the while documents that needed their signatures would be piling up.

"Hey, Molly, take care of the escrow."

"What's an escrow?"

"Fucking figure it out, stupid."

If I didn't get or do exactly what Reardon wanted, he would go crazy, and when he finally dismissed me, I would go home and turn off all the lights, get in the bathtub, and cry. Or I would drink wine with Blair after she had come home from being at an actual party with actual people, or on an actual date, and weep to her about my nonexistent social life.

"So come out," she would say, shaking her head at my stupidity. I wasn't even being paid that well; she couldn't understand why I was hanging on so tightly to something that was making me so miserable.

Blair didn't see what I saw. As much as I had intended on spending my year in L.A. being young, spontaneous, and carefree, my gut told me to stick it out.

I NEEDED TO STAY BALANCED, though, so I decided to volunteer at the local hospital. I wanted to work with the kids. Volunteering had always been important in my family, and my mom often took us to feed the homeless, or visit nursing homes. The children's ward felt very personal to me, because I had spent several months in and out of the hospital after my spinal surgery. I'd had very serious complications from the surgery. When I came off the operating table, my liver was failing and my gallbladder was severely infected. The doctors couldn't figure out what was wrong with me. They even had a theory at one point that I had contracted a mysterious infection while being cut open, so I was placed in the isolation ward. It looked like something out of a movie. The doctors wore hazmat suits and the whole ward felt like a giant bubble that I was trapped in. No visitors were allowed. I remember being afraid that I would die in there all by myself.

With the exception of those days in isolation, my mom never left my side. In the children's ward, it broke my heart to see how hard it was for the kids who didn't have that type of support. I was lucky enough to make a full recovery from my surgery, but the memory never left me.

Once I'd finished my training at the hospital, I began to spend a couple days a week after work with the kids who were terminally ill. We were warned that most of them would die, but nothing prepares you for the actual event. Despite being pale and weak, they were beautiful, happy little spirits. It was inspiring and humbling.

After a few weeks, I met a little girl named Grace, and despite her frail body, she was full of boundless energy and big dreams. She hadn't been outside in a very long time, and all she wanted in the world was to be an archaeologist, discovering lost cities. I begged and pleaded to be able to wheel her outside. Finally I got the approval.

I raced to the basement the following day, and her room was empty.

"She passed, Molly," my favorite nurse, Patrick, told me with a hand on my shoulder. Even though my supervisor had warned me about this moment, and asked that all the volunteers do their grieving in private and remain strong for the kids and their family, I lost it. Patrick walked me into the bathroom.

"It is part of the job. You have to be strong for the others. Take a moment," he said gently, and left me to sob on the bathroom floor.

While there was often heartbreak and tragedy, sometimes there were little miracles. One of the young boys, Christopher, was actually beating his death sentence and getting better every day. The light was coming back into his eyes and his paper-white skin was turning pink. He walked around the halls telling the other kids his story and giving them hope. Christopher's courage and optimism helped me maintain a healthy perspective in my new crazy world.

Chapter 4

Over time, and under the pressure of Reardon's forceful tutelage, I became the assistant who could do anything.

Skipping to the front of a waiting list for the latest overpriced watch, reserving a car during the New York City transit strike, one-night-stand removal: I could figure anything out. I could manage escrow accounts and secure reservations at restaurants that were booked out for months.

Now when Reardon asked for the impossible, I would just smile, nod, and call the restaurant.

"Hi, I'm just calling to confirm my reservation for dinner tonight."

"Sorry, we don't have it."

Pause.

"But I made this reservation ten months ago. It's my boss's birthday, and he flew his closest friends in from New York! Oh, my god, he's going to fire me. Please can you help?" I'd respond, adding some sniffles if needed.

Pause.

"What was your name again?"

"Molly Bloom."

"Okay, Miss Bloom. I see it here. Four people for eight P.M."

"Six."

"Oh, that's right. Six. Thank you, Miss Bloom. We're so sorry for the confusion."

ONE EVENING, I WAS FILING PAPERS, listening to the guys laughing and reminiscing in Reardon's office. Cam and Sam had grown up together, and Sam and Reardon had gone to college together. After finishing school, they realized that besides being great at partying together, they could build a company based on what each one brought to the table, and their partnership was born. Tonight they were in a great mood, celebrating another huge deal they had just closed.

"We like the Hunny, right, player?" asked Sam. "Hunny" meant money.

"Remember when you shot the moon man?" Sam asked Cam. "That was so roguish."

They laughed. I could hear them pouring another round.

"You have to tell Molly that story," said Sam.

My ears perked up, and I rushed into the room.

Cam stood up to better illustrate his tale. At 'six-foot-five, he was pure muscle, his energy was effusive, like a giant, out-of-control puppy.

"So we were playing paintball," said Cam, mimicking holding a rifle with which he shot each one of us. "My dad had Buzz Aldrin over, you know, that old guy who walked on the moon. So I walked right up to him and shot him, close range—BAM!" He continued to simulate the action. "And I said, *Boom, got you Moon MAN!*"

They all laughed hysterically.

I started laughing with them, picturing the absurdity of Cam blasting the legendary Buzz Aldrin with paintballs. "Pour little Molly a drink," said Reardon. "She helped with this deal."

"You're really starting to be a player, Mol," said Sam affectionately, and handed me a Macallan 18.

We all raised our glasses.

I wanted so much to be part of them. I wanted to make deals, to enjoy the good life that comes with money and status. The single-malt scotch tasted like gasoline, but I smiled and forced back my urge to gag.

THE BETTER I PERFORMED FOR THE BOYS, the more I was expected to do. But even as my responsibilities expanded, I was still responsible for Reardon's personal life. A big part of that personal life was keeping the high turnover of girlfriends happy. I was constantly being sent on high-end errands. I hadn't really been exposed or interested in designer clothes or handbags in my Colorado life. But the luxurious gifts I picked up for Reardon's girl of the week began to seduce me, and I started to imagine myself dressed in these clothes, wearing the beautiful shoes I delivered to Brittny and Jamie and whomever else Reardon bought consolation gifts for. It wasn't so much that I cared about these high-priced items, it was' that I realized people treated you differently, took you more seriously, when you had them. On this particular afternoon, Reardon sent me to a store called Valerie's.

It turned out that Valerie's was a high-end makeup shop in Beverly Hills that offered makeup application and custom blends for the who's who of Hollywood and Beverly Hills society.

I walked into the large door and it was like walking into a fairy princess land. Gauzy drapes, soft lavender hues, cream velvet chaises, and an array of beautiful products.

A beautiful blond woman greeted me. "Hi, I'm Valerie, how can I help you?"

"You did all this?" I asked Valerie.

"I created it all," she said.

"It's very beautiful," I replied longingly.

As she rang up the products Reardon had ordered, I almost choked— the tab was $1,000 for three things.

"Wow!" I exclaimed. "People really pay that much for makeup?"

She smiled, amused.

"Come here." She motioned me to follow her.

She led me to her station, which looked like an old Hollywood movie star's vanity. She whipped the chair away from the mirror and after just a few moments of brushstrokes, pencils, and mascara, she handed me a silver mirror. I was completely transformed.

It was unbelievable, like I was looking at a different person.

"Amazing . . ." I said, looking at myself.

"True luxury is worth the spend."

I nodded, catching another glance at my transformed face.

"Come back and see me when you're ready." She winked

And although I had been told my whole life that money couldn't buy you happiness, it was certainly clear to me that it could provide some desirable upgrades.

THE SALARY REARDON PAID ME covered the basics, but I decided I needed to earn some extra money to upgrade my wardrobe. To supplement my income, I applied for a part-time cocktail job.

Applying to be a cocktail waitress was a whole different world than applying for a regular restaurant job. For instance, most clubs ask for head shots.

When I applied at Shelter, I discovered that Fred, the manager, was the very eccentric former computer programmer from the first restaurant I'd worked at. L.A. was a town full of characters who were constantly changing roles. Take Fred, for example. One day he was in glasses and a skinny tie running seminars on restaurant operating systems; the next, he was the general manager for a caveman-themed club in an Armani suit. As soon as he hired me, he explained that my uniform would be custom made and slipped me a card. The designer's "studio" was a disheveled, tiny apartment in West Hollywood, and the designer himself was a colorful, flamboyant character who spilled his white wine spritzer on me as he took my measurements.

"All finished, my little peach!" he singsonged, and promised to call me when it was ready.

A couple days later my phone rang.

"Come over lovebugggg," I heard. "Hurrrrry! We want to have a fashion show!"

When I arrived, the designer's assistant handed me a glass of rosé and a small swath of material, and pushed me into a tiny bathroom.

I wiggled out of my clothes and changed into what was basically a skimpy faux–animal pelt with faux-fur trim. Back when I had taken the LSATs, I had never in a million years imagined that instead of power suits I would wear this getup. "Uh, guys, I think I need more material," I pleaded, too self-conscious to open the door.

"Don't be crazzzzy," the designer and his assistants called from the couches where they were lounging and sipping their wine. "You look amazzzzzzing."

To top it off, they handed me a clip-on Mohawk made from the same fake fur. I thanked them and they air-kissed me out the door.

One part of my brain said, *"You're going to look like a slutty rooster."* The other part said, *"Suck it up. The bottle service girls at Shelter make more in a night than you make in a week."*

THE MONEY AT SHELTER WAS GREAT. The success of the night was due to promoters, and the top club promoters had a loyal following of celebrities, billionaires, and models. On the biggest nights, people would wait outside the velvet ropes for hours begging to be let in. I got to know the promoters and eventually I was working the best nights at all the hottest clubs in town. A lot of the managers and promoters were sleazy alcoholics or drug addicts who leveraged their power over who got past the velvet ropes in order to hook up with the pretty young girls. The pretty young girls were almost all aspiring actresses or models, and they believed, truly believed, that getting into the club on the hot night would lead to their being discovered. The whole thing seemed silly, but I minded my business. I was punctual, responsible, and professional. While the other servers were doing shots and hanging out, I was making sure my tables were taken care of. My tips were always above 20 percent and I usually sold more than everyone else. I was there to make money, not friends.

Unexpectedly, my nights at this club furthered my L.A. education. Every night, I was dead sober, watching drunken Hollywood politick, hook up, and hang out. The money I made as a cocktail waitress allowed me to have a little extra, not enough to buy designer shoes but enough to upgrade my Colorado wardrobe. I also loved the way it felt to carry a rolled-up wad of cash home at the end of the night.

I was working long hours during the day, and at a different club every night. I was completely exhausted. But I discovered that I had endless stamina when it came to making money.

No matter how busy or tired I was, I never said no to a job.

Chapter 5

I had heard Reardon mention a place called the Viper Room over the last couple of weeks. Since I wasn't really allowed to ask questions, especially during the initial negotiations, I did my own research. I learned that the Viper Room was one of the most iconic bars in Los Angeles. Painted a matte black, tucked onto a seedy strip of Sunset in between liquor stores and a cigar shop, the venue had a rich history of celebrity and debauchery. I read that in the 'forties, Bugsy Siegel owned it, and it was called the Melody Room. When Johnny Depp and Anthony Fox took it over in 1993, Tom Petty played opening night, and River Phoenix had died of an overdose there on Halloween in 1994, while Depp and Flea played onstage.

I also knew that in 2000, Depp's partner, Anthony Fox, sued Johnny over profits, and while the suit was in progress, Fox disappeared. During the resultant confusion, the Viper Room was placed in the hands of a court-appointed receiver, who happened to be a family friend of Reardon's, and thus his company was given the opportunity to take over the Viper Room, which was then losing a ton of money, and to try to make it profitable again. I guess the deal was going through because one day, after Reardon yelled at people for his usual hour or so, he ordered me to get the car and directed me to the parking lot of the club.

As we pulled in, Reardon turned to me with a serious look on his face. "According to ticket sales and used inventory, the place should be profitable, but it's been losing money hand over fist for the past five years. The staff here is a bunch of scumbags; they've all worked here forever, and rumor has it there's been a lot of stealing going on. I'm probably going to fire them all, but I need you to get information from them, find out how the place works."

With that, he got out of the car and slammed the door so hard that I thought it would break. By the time I got out, he was halfway across the parking lot, and as usual, I found myself running to keep up.

We entered the black building through the side door. Suddenly sunny Los Angeles disappeared and we were in a sinister, dank cave, being greeted by a man with long hair, black eyeliner, and a top hat.

"Hi, Mr. Green. I'm Barnaby," he said, holding out his hand

Reardon ignored him and walked toward the stairs.

"I'm Molly," I said, taking the hand that was meant for Reardon and smiling warmly to compensate for Reardon's rudeness.

"Barnaby," he repeated, and smiled back. I followed Reardon up a dark staircase. The staff was seated around a table, and none of them looked happy.

"I'm Reardon Green. I'm running this place now. There are going to be a lot of changes around here. If you don't like it you can leave. If you want to keep your job you need to be cooperative and help make the transition smooth. If you guys can handle that, your job is safe.

"This is my assistant, Molly, she is going to spend some time with you today. I need you to show her how things work around here."

And he turned to leave. I smiled nervously.

"I'll be back in a sec," I said to the angry-looking mob.

"Reardon, seriously? You're leaving me here—what do you want me to do?"

"Just don't fuck up," he said, and he was gone.

I was suddenly hyperaware of my dumb sundress and cheesy cardigan.

I surveyed the angry faces in front of me. The staff members were speaking heatedly among themselves. They all wore black, most had tattoos and piercings, combat boots, Mohawks. They were rough, they were rock-and-roll, and I didn't know how to speak to them. I wanted to run out into the sunshine of Sunset Boulevard, but I took a deep breath and walked over to the angry crowd. The most important thing was to somehow figure out how to make myself relatable.

"Hey, guys," I said quietly. "I'm Molly. I don't know exactly what is going on. I wasn't given any information before Reardon left me here. But what I do know is that I can be an advocate for you. I work in the service industry too, at night, and during the day I try not to get screamed at or fired by the crazy man you just met. I usually fail at the getting-screamed-at part, by the way."

I heard a couple snorts, and even a little laugh.

"Anyway, if we can work together and give Reardon what he wants, I think we can all keep our jobs."

A woman in dark eyeliner and combat boots gave me a nasty look.

"You think you're gonna get what you need and then fire us all. I don't trust you one little bit," she said, jabbing a black fingernail scarily close to my face."

"Is that true?" asked an older guy with a goatee.

"I don't know," I answered honestly. "I can't give you a guarantee, but I can tell you that this is your best shot at keeping your job, and I give you my word that I will fight on your behalf."

"Give us a minute," said a pretty blonde in a short plaid skirt.

I walked across the room and sat down in a grimy booth, pretending to check my phone.

There was a heated discussion and two people walked out.

The rest came over to where I was sitting.

"I'm Rex. I'm the manager. Well, I *was*," he said, and held out his hand. The others introduced themselves.

I spent the rest of the day with Rex, who showed me how he ran the place while I took notes. I learned that he had a wife and a kid, and he had been managing the bar for ten years. He seemed like a really good guy. Duff was in charge of booking the bands and she gave me her master list, schedule, and explained how that process worked, and by the end of the day I had a fully functional operations manual, band and booker contacts, ordering information, and so on. I thanked them profusely and gave them my number.

"Call me anytime," I told them. "I'm going to speak to Reardon and tell him how helpful you have all been." I knew deep down that Reardon would probably fire them. I felt like an awful person as I trudged back to work. I walked into Reardon's office and gave him the notebooks. I went to my office and tried to think of the best way to present a case to give the folks I had met a chance.

He came into my office.

"Molly, this isn't good work," he announced. When I started to defend myself, he interrupted. "It's excellent." I was so shocked I almost fell off my chair.

"I'm proud of you," he said simply.

I had waited so long to hear any encouragement, some validation that Reardon didn't think I was the biggest idiot on the planet.

"About the employees . . ."

He turned around, his brown eyes flashing, the look he would give me right before he launched into a tirade.

"What about them?" he asked sternly.

"Never mind," I said, hating myself.

"You're coming out with us tonight. Be ready by seven. Really great job today."

I drove home feeling flashes of happiness followed by pangs of guilt.

The limo picked me up at seven, and all the guys were inside.

Reardon opened a bottle of champagne.

"To Molly, who is finally starting to figure shit out."

Sam and Cam echoed, "To Mol!"

I smiled.

We got out of the limo in front of Mr. Chow's, and paparazzi bulbs flashed as we got out.

"Look this way," they yelled at me, flashing their bulbs in my face.

"I'm not—" I began, but Reardon grabbed my arm and pushed the photographers away. We had a special table reserved for us, where we were joined by beautiful models, infamous socialites, and a few of Reardon's controversial but very famous actor friends. It was Friday night and every table at Mr. Chow's was reserved for the rich and famous. Every time I looked down I had a fresh lychee martini. We left Chow's and headed to the newest, most-impossible-to-get-into club in L.A. Everyone was buzzed, happy, and carefree. We sailed right to the front of the line at the club and were led to the best table.

I was so high from the drinks, the effortless glamour, the access, and the prestige that I almost forgot about the way I tricked the Viper Room employees into trusting me, used them for information, and then broke my promise to fight for them.

I grabbed Reardon's arm. I needed to at least try.

He smiled at me, his eyes full of pride.

And it was all I ever wanted, and it felt so good, so I let the employees and my promises fade away.

Chapter 6

ate afternoon on a Friday, I was shuffling around the office trying to get my work done quickly so I could leave early. I had a date with one of the bartenders at one of the clubs where I also worked. I would never tell the guys because they would make fun of me incessantly.

"GET IN HERE!" Reardon yelled.

I braced myself. He was doing the thing where he filled a yellow notepad with crazy doodles, something he did when he had a new idea. He would make geometric squares that connected and repeated until they filled the page. He had notebooks full of these—it was his way of working things out in his head.

"We're going to do a poker game at the Viper Room," he said, staring at the pad and scribbling away. "It'll be Tuesday night, you will help run it."

I knew Reardon played poker occasionally, because I had delivered and collected a couple checks since I started working for him.

"But I work at the club that night."

"Trust me, this will be good for you," He looked up from his pad. His eyes were smiling like he knew a secret.

"Take down these names and numbers and invite them. Tuesday at seven," he barked, scribbling his squares.

"Tell them to bring ten grand cash for the first buy-in. The blinds are fifty/one hundred."

I was scribbling furiously, I didn't understand anything he was saying, but I would try to decipher his words on my own before I dared to ask a question.

He started scrolling through his phone and calling out names and numbers.

"Tobey Maguire . . ."

"Leonardo DiCaprio . . ."

"Todd Phillips . . ."

My eyes widened as the list went on.

"AND DON'T FUCKING TELL ANYBODY."

"I won't," I promised him.

I stared at my yellow notepad. In my handwriting were the names and phone numbers of some of the most famous, most powerful, richest men on the planet. I wished I could reach back through the years and whisper my secret to the thirteen-year-old me, starry-eyed and love struck as I watched *Titanic*.

When I got home I Googled the words or phrases Reardon had used when instructing me to send out invites to the players. For instance he told me to tell the guys that the "blinds would be fifty/one hundred." A blind, I found out, is a forced bet to start the action of a game. There is a "small" blind and a "big" blind and they are always the responsibility of the player to the left of the dealer.

Then he said, "Tell the players to bring ten thousand for the first buy-in." The buy-in is the minimum required amount of chips that must be "bought in order for a player" to become involved in a game. Armed with a little understanding, I started to compose a text.

Hi, Tobey, my name is Molly. Nice to meet you.

LOSER! I thought. Scratch the "nice to meet you."

I will be running the poker game on Tuesday. Start time will be 7 P.M., please bring 10K cash.

Too bossy?

The buy-in is 10K, all the players will bring cash.

Too passive.

The blinds are—

Stop overthinking, Molly. These are just people and you are just giving them the details for a game with playing cards. I composed a simple text and pressed send. I forced myself into the shower to get ready for my date. I casually dried off, applied lotion, eyeing my phone across the room the whole time.

Finally I couldn't take it anymore. I raced over and picked it up.

Every single person I had texted had personally responded, and the majority had done so almost immediately.

I'm in
I'm in
I'm in
I'm in . . .

A delicious chill ran through my body, and suddenly my date with the bartender seemed very uninteresting.

OVER THE NEXT COUPLE DAYS I tried to figure out how to host the perfect poker game. There wasn't very much information on this subject. I Googled things like "What type of music do poker players like to listen to?" And I made mixes for the game with embarrassingly obvious song choices: "The Gambler" or "Night Moves."

While I tried out my new sound track to make sure it flowed, I tried on every dress in my closet. The reflection in the mirror disappointed with every attempt. I looked like a young, unsophisticated girl from a small town. In my fantasies, I would sweep into the game dressed in a fitted black dress from one of the most expensive stores on Rodeo, a sexy Jimmy Choo stiletto (Jimmy Choo's was Reardon's go-to for shoe gifting), and a strand of Chanel pearls. In reality I had a navy-blue dress with a bow in the back, and my navy-blue heels, a gift from Chad in college. They had certainly seen better days.

ON GAME DAY, I ran around doing errands for Reardon and the company, finding time in between to pick up a cheese plate and some other snacks.

The players texted me, almost compulsively, throughout the day. They wanted constant updates on who was confirmed. I felt giddy every time my phone lit up. It was like getting a text message from a boy you really liked, but even better. Reardon kept me late in the office to work on some closing documents for a new development project.

I barely had time to dry my hair and throw on a little makeup. I put on my disappointingly ordinary outfit and decided I would compensate for my lack of elegance by being superfriendly, helpful, and professional. I raced to the Viper Room with my mix tapes and my cheese plate. I tried to light some candles and place a few flower arrangements around the room to make it look more inviting, but it doesn't get much seedier than the basement of the Viper Room, and flowers and candles aren't going to change much.

Diego, the dealer, showed up first. He was dressed in khakis and a crisp white shirt, and he shook my hand and gave me a friendly smile. Reardon knew him from playing poker at Commerce Casino, a cardroom not too far from L.A. Diego had been dealing cards in casinos and home games for over two decades, and he had probably seen almost every scenario a card game could produce. But even his years of experience couldn't prepare him for how much this game would change all of our lives.

"You ready for this?" he asked as he unpacked a green felt table.

"Sort of," I replied.

I watched how quickly his hands moved while he counted and stacked the chips.

"Do you need any help?" I asked politely.

"Do you play?" he replied teasingly. "You don't look like a poker player."

"No," I answered. "This is my first time at a game."

He laughed. "Don't worry. I'll help you through it."

I breathed a little easier. I needed all the help I could get.

Barnaby showed up next, complete with his top hat. He was one of the only ones Reardon had kept on staff. He was manning the door; I gave him the list of names and stressed that he only let people on the list in.

"No problem, honey."

"Don't let anyone else in." I repeated myself several times.

"Sorry, Barnaby, I know you know what you're doing, I'm just so nervous. I want everything to be perfect."

He put his arm around me.

"Don't worry, angel, everything will be better than perfect."

I smiled gratefully. "I hope you're right."

AT 6:45 P.M. I STOOD by the front door and waited. I fidgeted with my dress. I started to feel insecure about how to greet the players. I knew their names, but did that mean that I should introduce myself?

Stop it, I said in my head. I closed my eyes and tried to calm myself down by imagining myself as I wanted to be.

"Molly Bloom, you are wearing the dress of your dreams, you are confident and fearless and you will be perfect." None of this was true, of course, but I wanted it to be. I opened my eyes, lifted my chin, and relaxed my shoulders. It was showtime.

The first person to arrive was Todd Phillips, the writer and director of *Old School* and the *Hangover* franchise.

"Hello," I said, warmly reaching out my hand. "I'm Molly Bloom." I gave him a genuine smile.

"Hi, gorgeous, I'm Todd Phillips, nice to meet you in person.

"Do I give the buy-in to you?" he asked.

"Sure," I said, eyeing the giant stack of hundred-dollar bills.

"Can I get you a drink?" I asked.

He ordered a Diet Coke. I went behind the bar and set the enormous amount of money down.

After I served him his drink, I started counting the stack. It was $10,000 all right. I put it in the cash register with Todd's name on it. I felt cool, edgy, and dangerous counting that much money. The others started to arrive.

Bruce Parker introduced himself and handed me his buy-in as well. I knew from my research that he had been a founding partner of one of the most prestigious golf companies in the world. Bob Safai was a real-estate magnate, and Phillip Whitford came from a long line of European aristocrats. His mother was a glamorous supermodel and his father was one of the most famous playboys in Manhattan. Reardon came blasting in with his typical "oh yeah!" greeting. The rumpled Houston Curtis showed up next, followed by Tobey and Leo. I straightened my shoulders and smiled as naturally as I could. They are just people, I told myself as butterflies flew manically around in my stomach. I introduced myself, took their buy-ins, and asked for their drink order. When I shook Leo's hand and he gave me a crooked smile from under his hat, my heart raced a little faster. To-bey was cute too, and he seemed very friendly. I didn't have any back story on Houston Curtis except that he was somehow involved in the movie business. He had kind eyes, but there was something different about him. He didn't seem to belong with this crowd. Steve Brill and Dylan Sellers, two more major Hollywood directors showed up next.

The energy in the room was palpable. It felt less like the basement of the Viper Room was a sports arena.

Reardon finished ripping into a sandwich and shouted to no one in par-ticular, but everyone in general, "Let's play."

I WATCHED, FASCINATED. It was all incredibly surreal. I was standing in the corner of the Viper Room counting ONE HUNDRED THOUSAND DOLLARS IN CASH! I was in the company of movie stars, important directors, and powerful business tycoons. I felt like Alice in Wonderland tumbling down the rabbit hole.

Diego fanned out ten cards and each player drew for their seat. There seemed to be a lot of weight being given to this action.

When everyone was seated, Diego began dealing the cards. I figured this was a good time to offer the players more drinks. I plastered on my brightest smile and went around the table offering drinks or snacks. Strangely, I wasn't getting the warmest reception.

Phillip Whitford grabbed my hand and whispered in my ear, "Don't talk to a guy if he's in a hand. Most of them can't think and play at the same time."

I thanked him graciously, and made a mental note.

With the exception of a few drink orders, no one spoke to me during the game at all, and I had time to watch closely. The ten men seated around the table were speaking openly. The movie stars and directors spoke about Hollywood, Reardon and Bob Safai analyzed the real-estate market. Phillips and Brill harassed each other constantly in hilarious fashion. Of course, there was talk about the game itself too. I felt like a fly on the wall in a top-secret, masters-of-the-universe club.

At the end of the night, as Diego counted each player's chips, Reardon said, "Make sure you tip Molly if you want to be invited to the next game." He winked at me.

As the players filed out, they thanked me, some kissed my cheek, but they all pressed bills into my hand. I smiled warmly and thanked them in return, trying not to let my hands shake.

When they were all gone, I sat down in a daze, and with trembling hands I counted $3,000.

But even better than the money was the knowledge that I now knew why I had come to L.A. I knew why I had withstood Reardon's temper tantrums, his constant insults, the degrading cocktail-waitress uniforms, the sleazy, ass-grabby guys.

I wanted a big life, a grand adventure, and no one was going to hand it to me. I wasn't born with a way to get it, like my brothers. I was waiting for my opportunity, and somehow I knew it would come. Again I thought of Lewis Carroll's Alice saying, "I can't go back to yesterday because I was a different person then." I understood the profound simplicity of that statement—because after tonight I knew I could never, ever go back.

Part Two
HOLLYWOODING

Los Angeles, 2005–2006

Hollywooding (verb)

To act in an exaggerated way in a poker hand, as a means of creating deception.

Chapter 7

I woke in the cool, dark morning before the sun and before my alarm, luxuriating in my sheets and letting my thoughts roll over the events of the night before. What a strange new world I had stumbled upon.

By the time I had finished cleaning up at the Viper, it was nearly 2 A.M. I had locked the doors behind me and run to my car with my purse tucked protectively under my arm. I drove home singing songs at the top of my lungs.

Blair was still out when I got home. I ran a hot shower, trying to calm myself down, but when I crawled into bed, I was still amped. I started making lists in my head of all of the things I could do with my tip money. Pay next month's rent. Buy some new clothes, pay my credit-card bill. I might even have enough to save a little.

I finally fell asleep.

When I climbed out of bed I immediately checked my sock drawer. The stack of hundred-dollar bills was right where I had left it.

I went to the kitchen to make coffee. According to the clock, it was barely 6 A.M., but the news was too good to hold in. I had to tell Blair. I had to tell somebody, or I was going to explode. She'd had a late night, so I knew I better have some coffee in hand.

"Why are you so happy?" she grumped, accepting the mug with her eyes half closed. I was about to burst out with the whole crazy, unbelievable story when the caffeine kicked in and reality sharpened into focus. Even though she was my best friend, and we told each other everything, I couldn't tell her this. It was my secret to carry, not hers. If she slipped up and told someone and it got back to any of the players, I would lose their trust.

I decided then and there not to tell anyone, not even my family, about the game. I wouldn't do anything to jeopardize my place in that room. "No special reason," I said, attempting to dim my enthusiasm. "It's just a beautiful day and I don't want you to miss it."

"Can't handle you right now. Shut my door." She groaned, and rolled over.

"Sorry," I said, stepping into the hall.

I GOT TO THE OFFICE early that morning, as I wanted to prove that the game wouldn't impact my performance. I spent an hour cleaning and organizing Reardon's desk and sorting files.

When I finished catching up on my work, I checked my phone. Seven new messages! My heart lurched. Usually that meant Reardon was raging about something. Not today, though. Today my in-box was full of messages from the players, asking me when the next game was, or commenting on how much fun they'd had. They also wanted to secure their seat for next week. I did a little happy dance.

Reardon didn't make an appearance until ten.

"Hi!" I said brightly, handing him his coffee and the mail.

"Someone looks happy," he said, with a wink.

I relaxed a bit; thank God, he was in a good mood.

"How much did you make?"

"Three thousand!" I whispered, still in disbelief.

He laughed. "Told you this would be good for you, stupid."

I beamed.

"Everyone loved it," he said. "They won't shut the fuck up. They've been calling me all morning."

I tried not to look too eager.

"We will have the game every Tuesday."

My face lit up and I couldn't control the huge smile spreading across my face.

"Don't let it fuck up your work," he cautioned.

Then he looked at my feet.

"And go buy some new shoes, those are fucking disgusting."

FOR OUR SECOND GAME, Reardon stipulated that all the players bring $10,000 for their initial buy-in and a check for any additional losses they might incur. Over the course of the week, as he fielded calls from people who had heard about the game and wanted to play, I listened carefully. I then created a spreadsheet for all the current and potential poker players.

I wanted to figure out how to be irreplaceable. I still had a lot . . . well, everything to learn about the game, but I knew a few things about human behavior from my time at the restaurants and watching my dad work. I knew that men, especially men of the social class and status of the card-players, wanted to feel comfortable and attended to. I upgraded the supermarket cheese plate to a swankier version from a Beverly Hills cheese store. I had memorized each player's favorite drink, favorite snacks, and their favorite dish from the high-end restaurant we usually ordered from. Those little details were sure to go a long way.

When Reardon gave me the finalized list of players I was to invite for the second game, there were nine of them, most repeats from the first game, and I set out to learn all I could about every one of them.

1. Bob Safai, the real-estate magnate. He was confident and he could be charming or terrifying depending on whether he was winning or losing. I had seen him berate the dealers and various opponents last week. He had been very nice to me, but I got the feeling this was someone you wanted to have on your good side.

2. Todd Phillips, the writer/director whose latest movie, *The Hangover,* had by now made its mark in the boy humor hall of fame.

3. Phillip Whitford, the aristocrat, was handsome, well mannered,

reeked of old money, and was arguably the best player at the table. He was the one who had given me the pointer about not speaking to a guy if he was in the hand, and had offered me encouraging warm smiles. I felt like he was an ally.

4. Tobey Maguire was married to Jen Meyer, daughter of the CEO of Universal. Despite his small stature, he was a huge movie star, and according to the guys, he was the second-best player in the game.

5. Leonardo DiCaprio, maybe the most recognizable movie star in the world. Not only was he devastatingly handsome, he was incredibly talented. He had a strange style at the table, though; it was almost as if he wasn't trying to win or lose. He folded most hands and listened to music on huge headphones.

6. Houston Curtis was the one that didn't belong. Houston had grown up without wealth or privilege. He was a producer of lowbrow reality content, such as *Best of Backyard Wrestling* videos. His claim to fame was that he had learned how to play cards when he was a little boy, and came to Hollywood without a dime. He seemed to be good friends with Tobey.

7. Bruce Parker was in his 'fifties. I heard him say he got his start by dealing weed. He had eventually leveraged his understanding of business to climb the executive ladder at one of the oldest and most successful golf companies. He allegedly made billions in sales and helped take the company public.

8. Reardon, who I already knew more about than I had ever needed to know.

9. Mark Wideman, whom I hadn't yet met, was a friend of Phillip's and would be new to the table this week.

This time, writing the text to the group was easier. I knew who they were and what to expect. I hit send, and just like last time, the guys responded immediately with *"I'm in"* and *"Who's playing?"*

I waited anxiously for Tuesday, and it couldn't come soon enough.

Chapter 8

Over the weekend I drove my beat-up Jeep Grand Cherokee to Barneys. I self-consciously handed the valet my keys, super aware that my car didn't exactly fit in with the sleek and shiny Mercedes, BMWs, Ferraris, and Bentleys.

Once inside, I forgot about my insecurities and I beelined for the shoe department. I looked around at the immaculate displays. For the first time in my life I could afford to buy whatever I chose. I was like a kid in a candy store.

"What can I help you with?" an immaculately dressed salesman asked, looking disapprovingly at the worn-out flip-flops I was wearing.

"I'm just looking," I said, ignoring his snobbery.

"May I pull some styles for you?" he asked.

"Sure," I said cheerfully.

After trying on ten pairs, I settled on a classic Louboutin black pump. "Are you this good at finding dresses too?" I asked him.

"Come with me," he said warmly, as I shelled out the thousand in cash to pay for the shoes. He was nicer to me now that I was spending money.

"Let me introduce you to my friend on the fourth floor," he said.

Her name was Caroline. Walking along with her, I felt like how my car must have felt in the lot with all of those fancier versions of what a car could be. I was incredibly aware of my own sloppy appearance. Barney's was filled with perfectly put-together women who looked like they had never had a bad hair day in their lives. I was in jean shorts, flip-flops, and a sweatshirt, my hair was in a messy ponytail, and I had on a Denver Broncos hat, but the worst was my glaringly obvious fake Prada purse that I had bought from a vendor in downtown L.A.

"How can I help?" she asked.

"I'm looking for a dress that makes me look nothing like myself." I laughed. She laughed too.

"Is this for work? Date? An audition?"

"With these prices, hopefully all of the above."

"I'm going to pull some options, so have a seat." She motioned toward the large plush dressing room.

"While I'm doing that, take off the hat, put your hair in a bun, and put on the new shoes."

I did as I was told.

She returned with several gorgeous dresses.

"Show me each one," she said.

I wiggled into a structured black Dolce & Gabbana. It was like a magic trick—it lifted my boobs, sucked in my waist, and accentuated my butt.

I walked out of the dressing room.

"Where did this body come from?" Caroline asked appreciatively, leading me to a three-way mirror. The dress created an optical illusion dress that made me look not only elegant, but sexy.

How could I say no, even to the price tag? This dress had transformed me as much as Valerie's makeup application.

"So there's your sexy, now let's get a classic, and you're well on your way to leaving the old you behind."

I smiled happily.

I tried on a navy-blue Valentino that hugged my body in the right places without being too provocative.

We finished the look with a strand of Chanel pearls.

"You sure are good at your job," I said admiringly.

She smiled. "Just give me your credit card and you will be on your way."

"Oh," I said, pulling out my wad of hundreds. "I have cash."

Caroline's face fell. I was sad. I could tell she thought I was a call girl.

"I'll be back with the total." Her voice was still friendly, just a little cooler. I was changing back into my clothes when she let herself into the dressing room.

"I'm not supposed to do this, it could get me fired. But I like you and I've seen this town destroy young girls."

"I promise you, Caroline, I am not an escort or anything like that. I just had a really good run at a poker game. And that's the truth."

She smiled. "That's very cool, and much better than the answer I feared."

"Here is my card, you call me anytime you need anything."

I smiled back. "Thanks for being honest, even at the risk of getting in trouble."

I walked out of Barneys with my new outfits, beaming from ear to ear.

FINALLY TUESDAY CAME, and Reardon actually let me leave work at a reasonable hour this time, so I drove home to change into my new outfit.

I was driving when my phone rang; it was one of my bosses from the club world. I was still picking up shifts when I could.

"Hey, T.J. What's up?"

"I need you to work tonight," he said. He sounded impatient. Everyone who works in the nightclub industry is always grumpy during the daytime hours.

"I can't," I said. This was the first time I had ever told him no.

"I guess you don't value your job," he said, his tone sharp. "There are a million girls in this town that would kill for it."

I thought about the money I had made last week working the game, more money in one night than I might take home in a month at the club, and I sucked in my breath and said, "Well, why don't you call one of them, because I quit."

He paused, shocked. I politely thanked him for the opportunity and hung up.

I knew I was being reckless. There was no guarantee this card game would last, but I was going to try to push it as far as I could. And it felt damn good to quit that thankless, demeaning cocktail job.

I SHOWED UP IN MY NEW DRESS AND SHOES. I had chosen the sexier one.

"Whoa, look at you," Diego said, taking the bags of liquor from me. "Your tips are gonna be gooood tonight."

"Is it too much?" I asked

"No way, you look hot, mama."

"Speaking of tips, what do you want to do about that?"

"About what?" I asked.

"Tips," he said. "The guys tip me throughout the game. I saw that they gave you some cash at the end. You're always gonna make more when there's chips involved. We can split if you want. Fifty-fifty."

I thought about this carefully. I had seen the guys throwing the chips into the center after winning a hand. So logic told me that ten guys tipping over the course of many hours probably translated to a lot of money, However, Reardon had made it clear that tipping me was the way to get invited back.

"Let's see what happens tonight and decide after the game." I wanted to see how much he made.

"Okay," he said, smiling.

Reardon walked in just then.

"Whoaaa," he said, laughing. "You kind of look like a piece of ass." That was as close to a compliment as I would ever get from him.

I squinted at him disapprovingly.

He looked at the food spread.

"Big-time!" he announced, and he tore into a sandwich. Translation: I had done well with my food selection. The truth was, I learned all of it from Reardon, who loved the best of the best, like caviar when he was hungover. I had come a long way since he had thrown Pink Dot bagels at me. All the food runs he sent me on, all of the cheese plates he ordered for the office, had impacted my awareness of the finer things.

Houston ambled in and gave me a warm hug.

I had his diet raspberry Snapple ready.

Bruce Parker was next, with Todd Phillips close behind him. He and Todd were laughing as they entered.

"What are you sickos laughing about?" Reardon said, fist-bumping. Reardon was a germophobe who opted to fist-bump instead of shake hands for sanitary reasons. Of course, his fear of germs seemed to fly out the window when it came to his sexual exploits.

"Parker just got a handy in the parking lot," Phillips explained.

"She was cute and only wanted five hundred, I figured it would be good luck." Bruce laughed.

"Roguish." Reardon nodded in approval.

Just then they noticed me trying to disappear into the corner.

"Sorry, sweetheart," Todd said.

"Molly's heard it all, she works for me." Reardon brushed off the apologies while I nodded and forced an easy smile.

"How does your boyfriend feel about you wearing that dress and hanging out with a bunch of scumbags like us?" Todd asked.

"I don't have a . . ." I began, but they had lost interest in me—Tobey and Leo had just walked in. The guys became a little shy, and awkward, except, of course, for Reardon, who fist-bumped Leo with a gruff, "What's happening, player?"

While the guys clustered around Leo, Tobey went over to Diego and handed him his Shuffle Master. The Shuffle Master is a $17,000 machine that is supposed to deliver a fair, random shuffle every time and increases the speed and accuracy of each game. Last week, Tobey had told the guys he wouldn't play without it.

The next player to arrive was Bob Safai. Last week I had watched Diego deal him what the others referred to as a "bad beat." This meant that even though Bob had a much stronger hand, he still lost. I watched as Bob had thrown his cards angrily at Diego.

Statistically, Diego had explained to me later, Bob should have taken the round. It was a "two-outer," which meant that there were only two cards in the deck that could make his opponent the winner. When Tobey hit it, Bob had gone berserk. He had given Diego a nasty look and said something about stacking the deck for Tobey. Incidents like that made me grateful that Tobey had brought a machine to shuffle this time, and that I wasn't dealing the games.

"Hi, honey," Bob said now as I took his coat. I saw his eyes flick around the room; even he got a little giddy when he saw that Leo was there.

Phillip Whitford walked in with his friend Mark Wideman. Mark was friends with Pete Sampras, who allegedly played high-stakes poker too. Wideman was a good player, but he had said he would try to bring Sampras, which would be a great draw for the game.

When he saw me, Whitford let out a low whistle and kissed my hand.

I blushed and looked at the floor, enjoying every surreal moment of being the only girl among such handsome, accomplished men.

And then above the buzz of voices came Reardon's ringing voice.

"Let's play!!"

THEY SETTLED INTO THEIR SEATS, and the air filled with the smooth sounds of my Frank Sinatra playlist, the whirring of the Shuffle Master, the shuffling of chips, and the happy playful banter of the players.

Once the game was well under way, it was hard to keep up. Guys were reloading their chips in rapid fire and everyone was betting all their chips at once, which Phillip told me during a rare pause was called "going all in." Even though I was a novice at poker, I was captivated. The game felt frenzied and exciting. And I wasn't the only one who felt the energy. Diego was dealing hands at lightning speed. The guys were also making side bets on the color of the flop (the first three communal cards dealt by Diego), and they even started wagering on sports.

I sat in the corner, always watching. Occasionally I would refill drinks. The guys were so focused on the game they almost forgot I was there, except for Phillip, who kept text-messaging me with poker insights. I typed furiously on my laptop, documenting everything I was learning.

Meanwhile, Bob was giving sound bites on the real-estate market, Wideman was talking about Sampras, Tobey was analyzing poker hands with Houston, Reardon was trying to get everyone on tilt by insulting them, Phillips was dropping one-liners, Leo had his headphones on to help him focus. Bruce talked for a while about the girl who had given him a $500 hand job, and then moved on to how he had made his money, beginning with his start as a weed dealer in Hollywood.

When it was time for dinner, I ordered Mr. Chow's. The guys weren't thrilled about the idea of stopping the game to eat, and I made a mental note to get side tables and, in the future, let them eat their food at the poker table. During dinner I heard Bruce ask Phillip where he should take a girl to dinner (not the hand-job girl, I presumed).

"I know the perfect place." I spoke up. "Madeo. Really romantic and the food is amazing."

"Great suggestion," he said.

"Want me to make a reservation for you?" I asked.

Thanks to all the reservations I had made for Reardon and the crew, I now knew the maître d's at all the top restaurants.

"That would be great." Bruce smiled.

"Bruce, text me when you want the reservation, and I'll take care of it."

"Thanks, Molly. You're the best." Over the last week I had been thinking of ways to insert myself into the players' lives, as I wanted to increase the chances that I wouldn't be replaced. I knew how much Reardon liked me to handle minutiae for him, so I had set a goal to try it with the guys at the table. I knew it had to seem natural, though, not forced. I felt it had gone perfectly well with Bruce. Later in the game I got a text from Houston, asking if I could get him and a friend into a certain Hollywood club. I knew all the promoters and doormen there, so I took care of that too.

THE GAME RESUMED AFTER DINNER at full speed. I sat in the corner watching Diego's hands fly around the table pushing chips and flipping cards—it was impossibly hard to keep up with. Suddenly the noise dimmed and Mark Wideman stood up. He walked around the table with his hands in his pockets.

There was a giant stack of chips in the center. My eyes traced the perimeter of the table to see who still had cards.

Tobey.

Tobey just sat there eating the vegan snack he had brought from home. His round eyes were fixed on Mark.

Mark deliberated while the rest of us held our breath. I had no idea what was happening, but I could feel the suspense.

"Call!" he announced.

Tobey looked at him in shock.

"Call?" he asked.

"Yes," Mark said. "Do I have you?"

I tried to add the chips up in my head, but there were so many and they were everywhere.

"You got me," Tobey said, and pushed his cards to Diego.

Tobey smiled at Mark. "Nice hand, man."

And then he looked directly at me, his eyes fixed in a hard stare.

"Who is this guy?" Tobey texted me.

Mark Wideman. He's an attorney.

"I see," was all he wrote back.

I had a sinking sensation that I was now in trouble.

The game picked up again and I held my breath whenever Reardon was in a hand and now Tobey too. I knew Reardon well enough to be certain that the thrill of the game wouldn't last long if he lost every time. Clearly I had to keep Tobey happy too. At the end of the night, they both came out ahead, but every second leading up to the last hand of the game was so full of anticipation that by the end of the night I was completely emotionally exhausted. But I loved every minute of it. The game lasted until 3 A.M.

As the guys filed out, I helped them with their coats and valet tickets, air-kissed and/or hugged good-bye, and was handsomely rewarded by each of them with cash or chips. I was immensely appreciative; I felt like it was so much more than I deserved. The biggest tippers were Phillip, Houston, and Bruce, who gave me especially large sums, but I made sure to thank each of them with the same amount of enthusiasm. Tobey, despite being the biggest winner, gave me the smallest tip.

Once they were gone, Diego and I sat down at the table. We combined our tips and then counted it out: $15,000. Seventy-five hundred each.

I looked at him in shock.

"Is this normal?"

"No." He chuckled happily. "I've never seen a game like this."

"Diego," I whispered. "Seventy-five hundred dollars! Are you freaking kidding me?"

"Just keep wearing those dresses," he teased.

I went behind the bar and poured us each a glass of champagne.

"This deserves a toast," I said. "To a fifty-fifty split as friends, and allies!"

"I like that," he said.

Even if our tips didn't always come to the same amount, it was nice to have a partner.

We drank our champagne in happy silence. Diego lived many freeways from Beverly Hills and had spent his career in inglorious casinos dealing bad beats to guys whose whole life could be ruined by the wrong card. He was in wonderland just as much as, or even more than, I was.

"I hope it lasts forever." I said, after a few minutes had gone by.

"Nothing is forever, especially in gambling," he said knowingly.

I forced Diego's words out of my memory. Instead, I heard my mom's voice in my head from every night when she tucked me into bed. "You can do anything you want, honey, anything you put your mind to." This may not have been what she envisioned, but it was what I wanted more than anything and I would do everything in my power to make it last.

Chapter 9

The follow-up to the games was always the same: Organize the players. Pay anyone who had won. Collect from anyone who had lost.

At first, the money part stressed me out. I felt bad asking the losers for money, and it took a lot of time to drive all over the city chasing and paying. But I soon came to realize that those one-on-one meet-ups were great opportunities to really get to know the men at the table.

On this particular Wednesday, I was scheduled to see Tobey and Phillip.

I went to Tobey's first. I was getting used to dropping by there: Tobey won every week.

I drove slowly up the steep drive, buzzed the security bell, and announced myself. "It's Molly, dropping off a check."

The long tone indicated that I had clearance. The gates opened slowly and I drove in. At the end of the driveway was Tobey's palatial house.

He was already at the door when I got there.

"Heyyyy, how are ya?"

"Hey," I said, handing him the heavy and awkward Shuffle Master. "Thanks for letting us use this for the game."

"No problem," he said, taking the machine. "I wanted to chat with you about something."

"What's up?"

His eyes squinted for a moment. "I think I'm going to start charging rent for the Shuffle Master."

I looked past him to the expansive foyer of his mansion in the hills. You could see straight through to the ocean.

I laughed. Surely he was joking. He couldn't possibly be serious about charging rent for a machine he insisted that we use, from the guys whose money he was taking every week.

But he was as serious as death, and I quickly stopped laughing.

"Okay," I squeaked. "Um, how much?"

"Two hundred dollars."

I smiled to conceal my surprise.

"I'm sure that will be fine. No problem," I said. I knew I should ask Reardon first, but I wanted it to seem like I was a decision maker. I would figure the Reardon piece out later.

"Greeaaat," he said. "Thanks, Molly. And there's one other thing. I'd like to know who's playing every week. If there's going to be someone new, I would definitely like to know who it is. In advance." His words came out slowly, sounding soft on the outside, but with a sharp-edged threat at the center. I figured this was probably about the hand he lost to Mark Wideman.

"No problem," I repeated, wanting out of there before I promised him my firstborn and my soul.

"All righty, talk to you later," he said, and waved a cheerful good-bye.

I shook my head as I drove away. I would never understand rich people.

PHILLIP WAS WAITING FOR ME at his favorite cigar club, which was discreetly tucked away in a two-story building in Beverly Hills. The elevator opened and I saw a lux mahogany foyer and behind it a smartly decorated lounge full of cigar-smoking men. I self-consciously checked around me for a sign that read NO WOMEN ALLOWED, but the maître d' smiled and led me to Phillip, who was sitting alone at the bar and sipping scotch.

He had a deck of cards in his hands, and he offered me a crooked smile.

"Just can't stay away from the cards."

"Actually, these are for you. I'm going to give you a poker lesson."

I blushed. Somehow I had hoped that the guys hadn't realized how little I knew about poker.

"How do you know I'm not a secret pro just hanging around to learn your tells?" I asked. Thanks to a Google search, I had learned a little poker vocab—tells are subtle changes in behavior that give clues to a poker player's hand.

He laughed appreciatively.

We moved to a table in the corner and I slipped him the envelope with his check inside. He took it, passed it close to his face, and then gave me a look.

"My poker winnings don't usually smell like flowers. Nice touch."

"I spilled perfume in my bag," I said lamely, embarrassed again.

His face went serious, and he shuffled the cards. Two for me, two for himself.

"These are known as pocket cards. Don't let anyone see them."

Poker is not so much about the cards you are dealt, but how you play the hand. You can win with a bad hand if you are able to read your opponent and understand what message your actions send, things like betting style or facial expressions.

He discarded one card he called the "burn card" and then laid three cards faceup in the middle of the table.

"Now, don't fall in love with a pretty hand, because when the flop comes, your pretty hand can become downright ugly. Poker is a game of odds, simple math, and being able to read people. If you are going to bluff, you have to believe it yourself. Keep in mind, the other players are looking for information from you. Facial expressions, body language, the amount and the way you bet. When you have what you believe to be the best hand, which is called the 'nuts,' you can either try to keep your opponents playing by betting in a way that strings them along, or bet aggressively and take the pot. And if you are going to go all in, make sure you have thought it through. Make sure you have the nuts, or that your opponent thinks you have them beat.

"But," he continued, "outplaying your opponent doesn't always work. Even the best players in the world have nights when they run bad. Recognize those nights and be disciplined with your downside, or the amount of money you allow yourself to lose. Know when to leave the table."

We tried a couple hands faceup as Phillip rattled out the calculations or odds of each of my starting hands and how they changed throughout the hand. After the flop (the first three cards), there was a turn (the next card), and finally a river (your last card). "I think I got it," I said.

The first few hands I played exactly the way he taught me. But after a while I got bored and I stopped folding even my bad hands.

He looked at me, disappointed.

"I don't think I'd make a good poker player. I'm too excited to see what comes next, even if I have a bad hand."

He laughed. "Don't forget, poker is much more than a game. It's a strategy for life. If you're going to be a risk taker, make sure you're taking calculated risks."

I nodded my head, taking it all in.

I drove to the office still thinking about the poker lesson. It seemed a lot more like a life lesson. I walked into the office, and before I could say hello, Reardon was rattling off an extensive list of things that HAD to be done ASAP.

"Pick up and sort the mail, pay the bills. And you have to unpack the boxes in the office. And I need more black shirts. And don't forget to file the docs and organize all the operating agreements, and you need to go to City National and drop off those forms, and . . ."

I nodded furiously, making notes as Reardon rattled off his lengthy list of demands. Since the game had started, he had substantially increased my workload. I started getting orders from him at 7 A.M. and sometimes it took until midnight to carry them all out. Except on game days, I was usually in the office or at his house, doing anything that needed doing. He knew he had ultimate leverage with me, and thus I indentured myself as Reardon's full-time slave in exchange for the right to be his part-time poker hostess.

For a full month, the game had gone off without a hitch. For four Tuesdays in a row, I had made thousands of dollars and listened to discussions on just about every pertinent topic from people in the know. The rich and famous were privy to information that regular people were not. I spent hours pondering the magnetism of the game, and the interaction between these men. Why did these guys, with their glamorous-seeming, full-to-the-brim lives, want to spend countless hours in a smelly basement watching random patterns emerging from a deck of fifty-two cards? They certainly weren't there to make a living . . . well, maybe Houston Curtis was.

After a month of listening and watching, I had a clue. For the most part, these were men who had risked it all to attain enormous success. Risked, past tense. Now they were coasting. They were safe. There was no jugular to their day-to-day lives. They could get any woman they desired, buy anything they wanted, make movies, live in mansions, acquire and disembowel huge corporations. They craved the adrenaline of the gamble: that was what kept them coming back. It was much more than just a game—it was escapism, adventure, fantasy.

It had become an escape for me as well. A way to avoid "growing up," which meant, at least to my father, succumbing to a life of thankless obligations. I decided that this game was the next level of my education. Everything that passed in front of my eyes was another lesson in economics, in psychology, in entrepreneurship, in the American dream.

So when Reardon said "jump," I jumped. That didn't mean I was happy about it.

"Is that all?" I said to Reardon with more than a hint of sarcasm. That day, he had just rattled off a week's worth of tasks with the expectation that I could somehow complete them all before I headed to Tobey's to deliver his winnings.

"Just one more thing," he said. "No more volunteering."

"Are you talking about the hospital?" I asked in disbelief.

"Yes," he said.

"What? Why?" I asked angrily. "It's never affected my job."

"That's not the point. I don't need you bringing germs back to the office. And you're too poor to volunteer. When you're rich you can volunteer as much as you want, but you're poor and stupid and you need to spend your time getting smarter and figuring out how not to be poor."

"You can't be serious," I repeated, waiting for an inkling of compassion.

"I'm dead serious. It's volunteering or the poker game. Your choice."

I stared at him in disbelief.

"You're not making any sense," I said. "You're being insane."

"Okay." He shrugged. "No game on Tuesday."

I stormed out of his office, my eyes watering as I thought about the smiles the kids at the hospital managed despite their situation. They deserved support and encouragement; they needed me and all the other volunteers. I needed them. I needed to feel like I wasn't completely losing myself in this new world of flash and money. It was selfish, I knew, but the reality check I got at the hospital helped keep me grounded and real. Reardon was always trying to make me tougher, and smarter; he equated idealism with stupidity. He kept me around because I worked my ass off, and I was the only assistant he had ever had that didn't quit after a week. He very rarely admitted it, but every once in a while he would tell me I had potential, that I could be smart. It was always followed quickly by an insult, of course. He was like an evil fairy godmother.

My volunteering was one of the last remnants of my former identity. An identity, I reminded myself, which went pretty unnoticed. Then I thought about the game. I thought about the flash and the high stakes, and the thrill of eavesdropping on the conversations of some of the most rich and powerful men in the world.

I had thought that I could be both idealistic and capitalistic, and one day I would be. But right now I was going to have to choose.

My old self hated my new self, but I willed her to silence as I typed an e-mail to my supervisor at the hospital.

After I sent it, blind-copying Reardon, I stormed into his office.

"Happy?" I asked.

He smiled like a Cheshire.

"Someday . . ." he said, "someday, you'll understand. Volunteering doesn't solve your problems. Every lost stupid girl I know is saving puppies or babies instead of facing the reality of what the world is and how to survive in it."

"You're evil," I said. "You're the devil incarnate."

He started laughing like a madman.

"I'm seriously worried about your soul."

"You're worried about my soul?" he asked, and laughed even harder. "Go worry about the soil reports for the new property, stupid."

Chapter 10

The poker game had taken off in a big way. The game had quickly gained the reputation as the best game in Los Angeles. The formula of keeping pros out, inviting in celebrities and other interesting and important people, and even the mystique of playing in the private room at the Viper Room added up to one of the most coveted invitations in town. I had to turn down important people every week. Soon we needed to host two games a week, and I was the gatekeeper.

The new faces at the table included:

John Asher, who spent half the time lamenting about his divorce from Jenny McCarthy and the other half getting made fun of ruthlessly by the other guys.

Irv Gotti (who was no relation to the Italian Gottis) who had started the record label Murder Inc and managed artists such as Ashanti and Nelly. He brought Nelly to a couple games.

Nick Cassavetes, son of Gena Rowlands, who had recently directed *The Notebook*.

A rich trust-fund kid named Bryan Zuriff, who gave off an air of being above it all.

Chuck Pacheco, who was one of the main members of Tobey and Leo's famed party crew.

Leslie Alexander, the owner of the Houston Rockets, and the occasional NBA player.

It was part of the fun each week to bring in a new face. It was kind of interesting to watch the dynamics. The new guy always felt awkward at first, and I tried my best to make him feel more comfortable. The regulars, especially Todd Phillips and Reardon, tried to make them feel uncomfortable. It was like watching a cliquish group of adolescent girls. If the guy started winning off the bat once he sat down, he was picked on even more. If he was losing or playing badly, the guys were much friendlier. If the new player was a celebrity or a billionaire, then all bets were off and he was treated like royalty.

You can tell a lot about a man's character by watching him win or lose money. Money is the great equalizer.

Sometimes there was miscommunication, and Reardon would invite someone without telling me and we would have too many players. In that case I would have to disinvite a man, and that was not a fun job. They often took it personally, yelling at me or throwing their status around.

"Do you know who I am?"

"Good luck getting my tip next time."

"I hope you have a plan B, because I'm going to get you fired."

I heard all these things, and it was hard not to get upset. But I realized the next time they were able to play that all of the bravado had been meaningless, because the hugs, kisses, and tips returned as the guy practically skipped to the table, happy to be one of the cool kids again.

And it wasn't just that every cardplayer in Hollywood wanted to come to the game, everyone's friends and their friends wanted to come to watch. I felt that a huge part of this enterprise depended on discretion, so I tried to discourage spectators when I could, but I couldn't stop the guys bringing girlfriends along to show off in front of, or the occasional celebrity stopping by. Celebrities were always allowed, to be honest. Like when the Olsen twins showed up with a billionaire I was trying to land for the game. They were in, no questions asked.

One night, Reardon sent me a text to go upstairs and bring his friends, who were waiting in the club, down for the game. I ran up as fast as I could—I didn't want to miss a second of the game. I recognized Neil Jenkins, tall and handsome, he jet-setted around the United States in his family's private jet. He was standing by the bar with a couple others, and I signaled for them to follow me.

As a general rule, I steered clear of Reardon's friends. They were generally all womanizers and I had heard way too many of their stories. I always pretended to be busy and not listening when these tales were tossed around, but I always took note. I didn't ever want to be spoken of or treated like one of the many girls they wooed and discarded.

I ushered the group downstairs and returned to my post behind Diego. I snuck a glance at Neil and his crew, noticing a guy I had never seen before. He was younger than the others and very cute. Our eyes met and I quickly looked away. After I made sure no one at the poker table needed anything, I asked Neil and his friends if they wanted drinks.

"I'm Drew," the cute new guy said.

"I'm Molly," I said with a friendly, but not too friendly, smile.

"Can I get you a drink?"

"Just a beer," he said.

There was something immediately comfortable about him. He could have been a guy I grew up with in Colorado. He was dressed casually, drinking Bud Light to his friends' Red Bulls and vodka. When I handed him his beer, our eyes caught again.

I scolded myself. Now was not the time. These were not the guys. I needed to focus on my job. I busied myself as much as possible with the game, but the game was busy with itself—there wasn't much for me to do. I sat down and pretended to work on my computer. Drew came over to talk to me.

He had recently graduated from Columbia with a degree in astrophysics. He was smart and funny and seemed worlds away from the shallow nonsense that most of these guys were obsessed with. I found myself smiling and laughing easily with him.

My phone buzzed and I glanced at it. It was Blair, demanding to know where I was.

It was her birthday and I had told her I would try to get out of work early, but I knew even when I had said it that it wasn't going to happen

I texted back my apologies, my promises to make it up to her, saying how sorry I was that I was caught up in something . . . the normal lame excuses.

She didn't even respond.

Phillip called me over, and then Bob needed my attention, and then Tobey wanted something, so I forgot about Blair and concentrated on the game. Meanwhile, I kept sneaking looks at Drew, wondering if I could make an exception to my rule about fraternizing with Reardon's boys.

When Reardon's friends got up to leave, I overheard talk of a strip club. Drew stood up to join them, and then glanced back at me. I waved cordially, disappointed that my theory was clearly wrong: he was just like the rest of them after all.

He came over to me.

"Hey, mind if I stay for a while?"

"Not at all," still pretending to be busy so he wouldn't see my big smile.

AT 2 A.M., IT WAS JUST REARDON AND ME, counting the stacks. I tried to sound nonchalant when I said, "So, Drew seems nice and normal."

Reardon rolled his eyes at me.

"He owns the Dodgers, stupid," he said.

"What do you mean he owns the Dodgers?"

"His. Family. Bought. The. Dodgers." Sometimes he liked to speak to me as if I were a two-year-old.

"Oh," I said. "Well, I didn't mean that I *liked him* liked him . . . I just thought he was an improvement over your other friends."

There goes that notion, I thought, conscious of my current low position on the social ladder.

Reardon gave me a knowing look.

My face turned red.

"Little Molly and Little McCourt," Reardon teased. "Anyways, he's dating Shannen Doherty."

Of course, he was dating one of the most notorious actresses in Hollywood.

"I told you. I don't care," I lied, and my heart sank a little more.

"Sure," Reardon said.

I concentrated on the money.

By the time I cleaned up and got out of there, it was 4 A.M., and I had missed Blair's birthday party completely. I felt terrible, but what choice did I have?

I let myself in quietly, hoping to not have to face Blair. She was sitting in the living room with a bottle of wine. Her face was red and blotchy.

"What's wrong?" I asked, rushing over.

"It's Jason," she said, starting to cry again. "We got in a fight and he left, and my best friend didn't even show up to my party. This is the worst birthday ever."

She buried her face in her hands and sobbed. She and Jason, her latest obsession, were constantly fighting and making up again.

I felt absolutely terrible. I went to her and rubbed her back. "Let's go to bed. It's late and everything will be fine in the morning."

She sat up, her face caked with black mascara and dried tears.

"Where were you?" she sniffled.

"Working." I sighed.

"What? What type of work keeps you there till three A.M.?" she whined.

"We have a lot going on," I said, which technically was not a lie.

"I feel so distant from you. It's like I don't even know you. We never used to keep secrets!" The hurt in her eyes broke my heart, but I didn't know what to say. I knew I was putting the poker game before my friends and family, but Blair had her trust fund to fall back on. I had to make my own way.

I couldn't go back to my old life. I was done struggling to get by. I was done being a nobody.

NO MATTER HOW EXHAUSTED I WAS the day after a game, people needed to be paid, and for that, other people needed to pay, and I was the collector. My first stop was Pierre Khalili. His luck the night before had never turned around, and he owed me a hefty six-figure sum.

Most of the time I dreaded making these collections. I realized that it was somewhat emasculating for the guys, because collections meant defeat, and these were not the type of men whose egos took kindly to losing, especially in front of a woman. I started to realize that there was a finesse to these collections, and I had been working on a few techniques to soften the blow. For instance, if I said, "Well, good thing you are so rich and handsome," with a look of admiration, most would smile smugly and hand me the substantial checks flippantly to prove my words were correct.

I wasn't worried about Pierre, though. He was a consummate gentleman. Raised in London, he hailed from one of the wealthiest families in Iran. He was cultured and sophisticated.

My phone rang while I was driving to Pierre's swanky Bel Air home. It was Blair, who had been sulking ever since her birthday.

"Hey, Blair," I said, hoping her bad mood was over.

"Brian called to invite me to Patrick Whitesell's Oscar after-party!!" she exclaimed. Brian was the actor she had dated before she started dating Jason. "Will you come? Please?"

"When is it?"

"Tonight," she said. "You'll come, right? You totally owe me, you missed my birthday."

Going to these parties was a mixed bag. They were glamorous, full of celebrities and fancy people, but they mostly made me feel inadequate and silly for being there. I usually ended up sitting in some corner with a glass of wine, wishing I was home.

But she was right, I owed her.

"You never come out anymore; you act all mysterious. I don't know anything about you! Are you a double agent? Is the CIA listening?"

I pulled up in front of Pierre's large ivy-covered gates.

"Of course, I'll come with you, but I have to go." I said trying to hurry off the phone.

"Yayyy! Okay, I love you. See you tonight."

I hung up and pressed the call button.

PIERRE'S BUTLER LED ME THROUGH the enormous house and into the backyard (more like back field it was so huge), where Pierre was sipping rosé and reading the paper.

"Darling, you look even more gorgeous than the last time."

I smiled, happily. I was always a sucker for a compliment.

He handed me an envelope, and by the weight I could tell it was all cash.

"I put a little extra in there for you," said the most gracious losing poker player in history.

"Pierre, you seriously shouldn't have," I protested. I honestly felt bad when people lost.

"I wanted to. You work hard and do a great job," he said.

"Would you like to meet me in Santa Barbara for a polo match this weekend? I'll send a helicopter if you don't want to drive."

I kept my gaze steady and tried to seem as if I received invitations like this all the time, but inside I was nearly bursting. I let myself imagine big hats, champagne, and what it would be like to ride in my own private helicopter. But then the voice of reason chimed in. It told me that getting involved with a player would not be wise. I liked Pierre as a friend, and clearly he was hitting on me. I couldn't lead him on.

"That sounds amazing, but I already have plans this weekend."

"Another time, then, darling. See you next week at the game?"

"Yes, definitely." I smiled, relieved he had been so gracious.

Driving home, I couldn't help but marvel at the way my life had changed in such a short time. I had been granted instant access to a world that I had never thought I would be a part of. I couldn't afford one misstep though. I knew it could all be taken from me as fast as it had been given. I knew I needed to be very analytical when these sorts of offers came along; I needed to think about things in the long term, not the short term. I needed to maintain the delicate balance between enjoying the fantasy of the game without stepping too far into the players' lives.

In years past, whenever I needed guidance, I would turn to my parents. My mother was so centered and full of principles and compassion, and my father's insights into human behavior often helped me navigate my way through unknown territory. But I hadn't told my parents about the game. It felt odd to keep secrets from Blair, but it was even stranger not to be telling my parents the truth about my life. It was creating a new kind of distance, one that had never existed before.

I suddenly had an overwhelming urge to talk to my mom. I wanted to tell her about some of the amazing things that were happening.

"Hi, honey," she said, answering the phone warmly.

"Hi, Mom, how are you?"

"I'm well, sweetheart. How are you? How is L.A.?"

"It's amazing, Mom, totally amazing. I'm really making it work. I'm making great money and meeting really important, powerful people, huge celebrities, and having so much fun," I gushed.

"That's great, honey, how's Blair?"

"Fine, the same," I said. "But, Mom, listen! This guy just offered to fly me to his polo match in Santa Barbara on his own helicopter."

"That sounds exciting. How's Christopher? Did he finish his chemo?" she asked, referring to one of the kids from the hospital.

"Um, I don't know. I took last week off," I lied.

"Well, you'll find out next week and let me know," she said.

"Sure," I said.

The delicious lightness I felt a moment ago became a heavy feeling of guilt.

Meanwhile, Todd Phillips was calling me on the other line, probably wondering where his share of Pierre's money was.

"I have to go, Mom," I said.

"Honey, are you okay? You don't sound like yourself."

"I'm fine," I said. "Everything's great. I just have to go."

The distance between us broadened.

"Love you," she said.

"Me too," I said.

And I clicked over to Phillips.

THAT EVENING, I changed out of my jeans and sweater into my new black dress, along with my strappy Louboutins.

"Wow," Blair said. "Where did you get that dress?"

"Hand-me-down from one of Reardon's girlfriends." Wow, that lie came quick and easy, I thought. I felt compelled to downplay everything now, every detail, so that I wouldn't have to answer questions about what I was doing for money.

What I wanted to say was, *"I BOUGHT IT MYSELF, ALL IN CASH! . . . And I text with Leonardo DiCaprio and Tobey Maguire, and I have twenty thousand dollars in my closet!"*

But I couldn't.

WHEN WE ARRIVED AT THE party, stars were posing on the red carpet and paparazzi were swarming. The moment we walked into the house, Blair found Brian.

"Mol, I'll be right back. Brian wants to show me the view from the roof." She giggled and winked at me.

I smiled and nodded weakly.

Really, BLAIR?

I sighed and grabbed a glass of champagne off of a silver tray. I waited for Blair for a bit and self-consciously pretended to be texting on my cell. After a while, Blair was still missing, so I wandered around the house, which was enormous, cold, and full of A-listers—statuesque models and buxom Playmate types. Outside, on the deck, I sipped my drink and admired the way the city sparkled below.

I thought being here would feel different in a new dress and proper shoes, but Hollywood was a lot grander than a new pair of shoes. The biggest stars in the world orbited this planet, and coexisting with them was a daunting proposition. I was used to the sensation of inferiority, having grown up with my superhero brothers. I just wanted something that was all mine. There were two men chatting on the patio, and I must have been as invisible as I suspected because they didn't even acknowledge that I was there. One was a big director that I recognized easily, and the other was the well-known head of a talent agency.

"Will he do it?" the director wanted to know.

"He's already agreed to the number."

"How do you know?"

"My boy played with him in the Hollywood game."

"What game?"

"The Secret Poker game."

My ears perked up.

"It's superexclusive. You need a personal invite and a password."

I giggled at the password exaggeration.

"Are you serious?"

"Nobody knows where they play. Nobody who plays will talk about it. But everybody knows about it. And everybody wants in."

"Who runs it, how can we get in?"

"Some girl. She controls the list."

And then it struck me that I *could* have everything that I wanted. There was no reason to feel sorry for myself, to feel inferior anymore—I had ultimate access. Business deals, movies, takeovers, mergers . . . the sky was the limit. I just needed to continue feeding it new, rich blood; and to be strategic about how to fill those ten precious seats. Recruitment for this game was crucial, and though I didn't really control the list, it was the illusion that I did that mattered. From my hundreds of hours of watching the guys play, I felt confident in my ability to bluff. I downed my champagne and approached the two men.

"I couldn't help but overhear you," I started.

They both blinked at me, trying to decide if I was a mere peasant or someone they should be nice to.

"I'm Molly Bloom and I run the game you were referring to. If you give me your cards, I can get in touch if a seat opens up." Suddenly these two powerful men were fumbling like mad to produce a card.

They started asking me a barrage of questions.

"Who plays? Where do you play? When's the next game?"

I stayed quiet and coy. "I'll be in touch, I promise." I shook their hands and sauntered off. I could feel them watching me walk away.

Chapter II

Christmas rolled around, and it occurred to me that I hadn't been home in two years. My schedule was incredibly demanding, between Reardon's ever-increasing needs and the game. I sensed that the looming housing crisis was taking a toll on the real-estate business. Reardon was even more stressed out and difficult than usual. I was at his side every day, and I often felt like his punching bag. I had become accustomed to the constant stress, minimal sleep, and basically living in a constant state of fear that I would lose everything. There was nothing stable about my life; I was completely beholden to Reardons whims. I knew that if he decided the game wasn't serving him anymore, he could end it. I had spent the last year carefully inserting myself into the players' lives, becoming a one-stop concierge for all their needs, in and outside the game. It was like having fifteen Reardons in my life, but I didn't mind. After the Oscar party, I had overcome my shyness around people who were successful, famous, or any of the other attributes that made them a good addition at the table.

It still wasn't easy to find the right players for the game, despite my having overcome my fears. First, I had to be discreet. Second, I had to make sure the player actually had the money he claimed to have (if you knew how many people in L.A. drove Ferraris and wore diamond-encrusted watches but had no cash or assets, you'd be shocked). Third, I had to make sure they weren't very good players, and finally I had to make sure all of the very opinionated, critical elitists of the core group would approve of them. In the beginning, I managed to recruit lots of "fish," or bad players, in poker parlance. The first night they played I was stressed to the max hoping my fish would lose, be amicable, and the other guys would like him. And then, if he did lose, I was stressed again hoping he would pay. The core guys all really liked me, treated me with respect, and allowed me to be in charge of their money. I couldn't do anything to betray their trust.

Reardon, on the other hand, was harder to win over, even though I had been at it longer with him. I still felt like I had to prove myself to him every day. He was hard on me, even though deep down he believed in me. I had avoided going home because I knew he would see my missing my family as a sign of weakness, and I knew very well what Reardon thought of weakness. But this year, I decided to take a chance. Reardon said he was fine with it. I knew he wasn't, but I chose to believe him—I felt I had earned a break.

I flew out on Christmas Eve and my mom picked me up at the airport and took me straight to the Denver Rescue Mission. It was a family tradition to serve dinner to the homeless on holidays. I felt different this year. I still felt terrible for the folks at the shelter, but I also felt a bit detached. I spent the whole night checking my phone.

"Honey, why don't you put that thing away for a while?" my mom eventually said . She was right. I put my phone in the car and tried to be present. It was the first time I had walked away from my phone for more than a minute since I started working for Reardon. I literally slept with the thing on my chest.

When we got back to the car, I had five missed calls and several new text messages. My stomach lurched and the familiar anxiety returned. It was Reardon, fuming about everything. The television didn't work. I hadn't set it up properly. There were a million things to do in the office and I hadn't gotten them all done. He needed dinner reservations and he needed me to get in touch with one of the construction teams and why the hell wasn't I answering my phone? I called Comcast and confirmed that they were having some issues, and the whole area was without cable. I called Reardon back and communicated the message. But he didn't want to hear a reasonable explanation. He wanted to punish somebody. So he yelled and ranted while I sat in the car with my mom and my brothers. They could all hear his tirade. I was beyond embarrassed.

"This will be another fine!"

Reardon had recently taken to fining me when I didn't do things "correctly." The worst part was that he wasn't even paying me through the company anymore. First my salary had decreased once we started the game, even while my hours increased. As my tips from the game grew, my salary had been completely abandoned. Now my tips were my only source of income, so being fined by Reardon didn't mean having my pay docked, it meant digging into my own pocket.

Reardon had recently moved into a new house and he had kept me working until midnight every night before my trip home packing and unpacking boxes. Apparently I hadn't done a good job packing a marble shelving unit that the previous owner had wanted to keep.

"YOU don't care because it's not yours; this shit would cost me a lot of money if it broke. You just half-ass it. Well, now you're going to care. I'm fining you a thousand dollars. Now get back over here and do it correctly."

Every time I protested a fine, or pushed back at all, he would threaten to take the game. I just accepted this as part of the fabric of my new life, like having to pay the troll to cross the bridge.

"I can't control your local cable networks, Reardon," I said.

He screamed louder: "You suck at everything these days, you don't care, and you don't give a shit."

"Reardon, I do care, I go above and beyond, but I am with my family and I can't talk about this right now. I have to go," I said.

And for the first time since I started working for him, I hung up before he did.

MY BEDROOM WAS JUST AS I'd left it two years ago when I drove to L.A., maybe a little cleaner. It seemed like a lifetime ago that I had gone, but here were all of my things, as familiar as if I had never left. I sat at my desk and looked around, taking it all in. When the phone started to ring, I didn't want to answer, but I was more afraid of the drama that would ensue if I ignored Reardon than the tirade I would hear when I picked up.

"Hi, Reardon," I said.

"You're fired," he said.

"What?"

"No more game."

"Are you serious?" I said. "You're firing me on Christmas Eve? Because Comcast is having service problems?"

"Let me phrase it so that you can understand me," he said. "You're fired. Merry Christmas."

And then I heard a dial tone.

Reardon had fired me before, sometimes on a daily basis, but this was a whole new level of cruel. I spent the whole evening feeling distracted and stressed. My stomach was tied in a million knots. I had so wanted to show up in my fancy new clothes, regale everyone with interesting stories from my new life, maybe even pick up the tab for dinner and then dash back to the airport leaving them all with no doubt in their minds that I was successful and happy. But instead, here I was, being ordered around, demeaned, and screamed at for my whole family to hear.

"I don't get it," my brother Jeremy said confusedly. Jeremy the Olympian, Tommy Hilfiger model, golden boy. His athletic ability and marketable face had allowed him to skip out on unglamorous jobs in the real world.

"You're better than this," my other brother said.

It was hard to explain to them, but I had my vision of my life etched in my mind and Reardon's temper tantrums were a necessary evil. They understandably did not appreciate what controlling this poker game could mean. Forget the money, which was great and life-changing, but the network, the information, the access. Poker was my Trojan horse, I could use it to penetrate and access any part of society I wanted. The art world, finance, politics, entertainment. The list was endless. I had realized that it didn't matter that I wasn't stupidly brilliant at one thing—I was great at recognizing opportunity. I had an entrepreneurial spirit and these games were a gold mine of opportunity. Not to mention I got to learn from some of the world's masters of their trades. So maybe my parents, or my brothers, or Blair didn't understand, but I did. I needed to smooth things over with Reardon, but I wanted to let him cool off.

I called him the next morning figuring he would act as if nothing happened like he usually did, and dole out new orders. But his voice was different, he sounded very serious.

"I am going to have a new girl run the game. She will be calling you today. If you get your shit together you can come back to work on Monday, but only as my assistant. No poker."

"Reardon, that's not fair, I come to the office at seven A.M, I leave when you tell me, sometimes around ten P.M. If I make mistakes they are small and insignificant. I run your life and I am the only one helping you run the company."

"The choice is yours, you can have your job back if you want, but I've made my mind up about poker. This conversation is over." He hung up.

How could he do this to me? My heart was pounding. I felt like I had ice water in my veins. "I'll figure it out, I'll fix this, he will come around," I told myself.

My phone rang again, I didn't recognize the number.

"Molly?" said a female voice.

"Yes," I said.

"Hi!" It was the new girl. "Reardon asked me to call you to get the names and numbers of the poker players . . ."

My anxiety turned to white-hot anger. There was no way I was letting this happen.

"I'm going to have to call you back," "I said through gritted teeth. This time I hung up.

I took a deep breath. I needed to think. I needed to be strategic. I had learned from watching the guys play that it was the calm, cool, unfettered heads that prevailed. Playing a hand or making decisions motivated by emotion rarely yielded a positive outcome.

The odds were clearly stacked against me. Reardon was part of the billionaire boys' club. He gambled with the players, spoke their language, and many of them feared him. I, on the other hand, was the girl who served them drinks, laughed at their jokes, did favors for them—and was always nicely compensated. And in their minds, I belonged to Reardon. I needed an ally who was as powerful as, or more powerful than, Reardon and who would actually stick his neck out for me. The clear choice was Phillip Whitford. He had power, clout, integrity, and we had become very close friends. I called him and explained the situation.

"He can't do that," Phillip said, quietly but firmly. I wanted to stay composed but it was just so unfair, and explaining it to Phillip made me so angry at the injustice that I started to cry a little.

"Molly, don't cry. We will fix this. Here is what we are going to do."

Phillip proposed having the game at his house with all the players except Reardon. He would talk to the guys about what Reardon had done and he would try to convince them to let me officially take over the game.

It was a long shot, but it was my only shot.

"MOLLY, C'MON, WHAT IS TAKING SO LONG?" my brother Jordan shouted from downstairs. We had planned a day of skiing, just my two brothers and I. It had been a long time, maybe six or seven years, since that had happened. I was looking forward to it.

I WAS QUIET IN THE CAR on the way to the mountain.

"Mol, what's up? You haven't been yourself this whole trip."

"Sorry, I'm just stressed with work and stuff," I said, and forced myself to sound jovial.

We rode up the lift, fighting over whether or not to have the bar up or down as we had done so many times as kids. We decided to make our way to the run—Ambush—where we had all learned to do moguls. Standing on the top of the lip looking down at the steep field of bumps, I could almost see my dad there, in his red jacket, leaning on his poles and screaming at us to keep our knees together. I remembered the first time I had stood in this place after my surgery. It had been months since I had been out of bed, much less on the slopes. That had been the most meaningful run of my life. Everyone had counted me out, but I got back on my skis. I made the U.S. Ski Team, and I got to wear the jacket, and stand on the podium with a medal around my neck. I don't know if any of that would have felt as good if I hadn't had to work so hard, to defy odds to get there. I smiled to myself, and calmness washed over me. I had nothing to lose, and so much to gain. I felt free and alive.

I watched my brother Jordan go first; he was still an incredible skier. He had always been a major talent but he had given up skiing competitively a long time ago to follow his dream of going to medical school.

Jeremy went next. Jeremy was number one in the world and was currently on a winning streak that no other skier had matched. Watching him ski was mind-blowing. He was my little brother, but he was also the best skier in the world. He was also currently the star wide receiver at the University of Colorado. I was proud and inspired by my brothers because they hadn't simply relied on their natural-born talent. They trained or studied harder than their competition, they treated failures as opportunities to get even better. I suddenly felt confident and inspired. I pushed off with my poles and pointed my skis fluidly through the deep rut line.

My brothers cheered.

"You still got it, sister," Jeremy said proudly.

I smiled widely and pushed L.A., the game, and Reardon out of my head.

Chapter 12

Everyone had confirmed for Tuesday's game, everyone, that is, but Reardon, who had not received an invite. He wasn't arriving back from his holiday vacation until late on Tuesday, and before he had fired me and tried to replace me, he asked me to send invites out for a Thursday game only, so that gave me a small degree of comfort.

I arrived at Phillip's to set up. His house was elegant, with the rustic undertones of a writer's retreat, all burnished wood and jam-packed book-shelves. His backyard was expansive, wooded, and featured a vine-covered trellis. It all had the feel of something from a Fitzgerald novel. The whole house was elegant and understated, the opposite of the too-much-money-too-little-taste that most L.A. homes reeked of.

I tried to appear composed, but on the inside, I was a mess. If tonight went badly I would lose everything. But if my plan worked, not only would the game be mine, but I would be free of Reardon's oppressive hold. I was going all in, and it was terrifying, but electrifying too. Suddenly I felt an intimate bond with the players and the game.

Phillip smiled at me when I arrived.

"You look beautiful. This is going to work," he assured me.

I smiled and gave him a hug.

"Thank you for what you are doing," I said. I knew this was a risk on Phillip's part. Reardon was a formidable enemy.

THE PLAYERS BEGAN TO ARRIVE. Bruce Parker, Steve Brill, Todd Phillips, Tobey, Houston Curtis, and Bob Safai; it was a full house. Tobey was the only one who knew about my scheme.

They all seemed thrilled to be in Phillip's beautiful house, which was in stark contrast to the dark and seedy Viper Room basement. I could tell immediately they felt much more relaxed and comfortable here.

If I take the game over, I told myself, I'll clean it up. Upgrade. I imagined holding my games in beautiful rooms, with snack tables outfitted with caviar and fine cheeses. I would hire beautiful girls to quietly serve drinks, and the city of Los Angeles would twinkle many stories below my poker penthouse. If these boys were looking for escapism, I would take them all the way.

"Where's Reardon?" asked Todd.

My heart was in my throat.

"He's not playing tonight," Phillip said, sounding casual.

The game started smoothly; I was gratified to see that everyone was having a great time. The only one who looked unhappy was Phillips, who claimed to prefer seediness to the comforts of a lovely home. Phillips was by nature a contrarian and a general troublemaker, which was completely forgivable on account of his dry wit and comedic timing. His brand of humor was dark and caustic and literally had the table in tears on any given night, which is a huge value add at any poker game.

When dinner arrived as usual from Mr. Chow's, the men opted for a civilized meal as opposed to eating at the table as befitted their surroundings. I arranged the dining room, and they descended on the spread like people who had never seen food before, giving me a second to take a breath. I wandered outside into the fragrant garden. I sat on a carved bench looking up at the sky. The sun was setting and it was that time of day when the light is perfect and the edges soften. Through the French doors, I could see the guys talking, laughing, and gesticulating with their chopsticks.

I want this to work so badly, more than I have ever wanted anything in my whole life. I sat quietly in the garden, periodically checking on my players. I needed to clear plates if they were finished eating. They seemed to be having a serious conversation. My entire body froze. I took a lap around the garden, and when I returned to the bench, I saw Phillip walking toward me. His hands were in his pockets and he was looking down.

"I lost it, didn't I?" I asked, feeling like I might throw up. It was a risk, and a calculated one, just as Phillip had taught me. I started babbling, telling myself it was just a game. I'd be okay.

"Molly, MOLLY," he said loudly, stopping me.

"You won, the game is yours," he said.

A shocked but huge grin spread across my cheeks.

I threw my arms around Phillip and hugged him so hard he laughed.

In fact, it had been a unanimous vote.

"You're a good, good man, Phillip Whitford," I said, smiling.

I floated through the rest of the night. Along with my tips that evening, I received a chorus of personal promises to stick by me. Everyone liked Reardon, but they didn't think he was right to cut me out. Phillip opened a special bottle of champagne when everyone had gone. We sat together on his back porch.

"Why did you help me?" I asked.

"It wasn't fair and I'm a sucker for the underdog."

I smiled and drank more champagne.

Suddenly I remembered I had to contend with Reardon.

"It's not over yet," I said. "I still have to face Reardon."

"Do you want me to talk to him?" Phillip offered graciously

"I have to do this alone, but thank you a million times for offering."

I knew Reardon would find out soon enough. And, although the players had pledged their allegiance to me, I had been around this crew long enough to know that I couldn't rest easy.

I got home around three thirty. I lay in bed, sleep eluding me.

MY PHONE STARTED TO RING at five thirty the next morning.

"Get over here," Reardon growled. I had heard him angry, but never like this.

"Coming," I answered, to nobody. He had already hung up.

I got ready quickly and jumped in my car. The early-morning stillness and the lack of traffic on Sunset made me all the more anxious. The view outside my window went by in slow motion. What was Reardon going to do to me? He went so crazy over the smallest things, what would he do with this? Hurt me? Force me to leave L.A.? I couldn't even imagine.

I pulled into his driveway and sat in my car for a minute. My face in the mirror looked wan and fearful. You have to face this, I told myself. I took a deep breath and got out of the car.

Reardon made me wait for a few minutes before he answered the door.

"Go wait for me in the guest room," he said, in the most serious tone I had ever heard him use. His brown eyes were narrowed to slits, and in the half-light of the dawn, they looked almost black.

The guest room was all the way in the back of the house. I had no idea why he was sending me there. Still, I made my way in that direction obediently, and then I waited. Five minutes. Ten minutes. My anxiety was growing and I felt like I was going to pass out. I focused on breathing deeply but the breath wasn't getting past my throat.

Do I let him talk first? Do I assume a tone of strength or passivity? I sat on the bed with my knees folded up under my chin. I didn't feel strong. I felt like a little girl waiting in the principal's office. At this point I just wanted him to get whatever he had planned over with. What had I been thinking? My plan seemed so stupid now. Reardon would never let me get away with this.

He finally came in, interrupting the noisy escalation of my thoughts, and took a seat across from me. He didn't speak at first, just stared, hard and emotionless.

I stared back, as evenly as I could, and tried not to cry. I was about to break down and beg him for forgiveness, promise to come back to work, and walk away from the game completely when I heard his voice from a far-off place.

"I'm proud of you."

Clearly I had misheard.

"I'm proud of you," he repeated, and started grinning.

In none of the scenarios I had envisioned was the dialogue anything like this.

"You are?" I asked, ready for him to recant and start screaming at me.

"I am," he said. "The game is yours. You earned it."

I shook my head in disbelief. I couldn't be this lucky. Things didn't work out like this in real life. I saw Reardon was smiling at me like a proud father.

My whole body relaxed, maybe for the first time since I had moved to L.A., and a huge grin spread over my face. I had never felt so happy, or been so shocked.

I jumped up and hugged him, for the first time since I met him.

He laughed and shrugged.

"You deserve it, stupid," he said. "You're a great student."

I HAD ARRIVED, I had the game, I had Reardon's respect, it was almost 2006, time for a new year, a new me. I felt like it was my graduation day.

Reardon patted me on the head.

"Little Moll is growing up," he said, looking at me with a sense of pride. He switched gears quickly.

"What should we do for New Year's? We need a roughish plan."

Part Three
PLAYING
THE RUSH

Los Angeles, 2006–2008

Playing the Rush (noun)

A series of results in a game of chance that work out in a gambler's favor, within a relatively short time frame.

Chapter 13

In an ironic twist, Phillip, Reardon, and I decided to go to Miami together. It was almost an open gesture of peace and concord. Phillip and a couple of his friends from the exclusive private school he had attended as a kid had chartered a yacht for the week. We all purchased first-class tickets. It was the first time I had ever flown first class. I couldn't believe the difference. The usually stone-faced flight attendants smiled and tucked me into a giant plush leather seat and brought me a glass of champagne. I looked around at the other passengers to see if they were as excited as I was by this royal treatment. They looked bored. I started pressing buttons and the seat turned into a bed. I looked incredulously at Reardon. He laughed. I turned and looked at the coach passengers crammed into their tiny seats and I decided I never wanted to be back there again. The flight attendant then showed me the in-flight entertainment, where I could watch every single current film. When we arrived, a driver was standing at the baggage claim holding a sign with Phillip's name. He carried our bags to his slick new black Mercedes and informed us the ride wouldn't be too long. We arrived at the Marina and a member of the crew met us. The marina was full of large, fancy yachts.

"Which one is ours?" I asked, after introducing myself to the guy.

He pointed toward a navy-and-white yacht that looked as big as a cruise ship.

My eyes flew open. Suddenly I felt insecure. I was sure everyone else on the boat was fully accustomed to this lifestyle, and I didn't want to seem like the one that didn't belong. I curbed the skip in my step and tried to feign boredom as I had seen the other passengers in first class do.

This boat was incredible, unlike anything I had ever seen. It was a fully functional floating mansion equipped with a formal living and dining room, a gym, even a helicopter. As I assumed, my fellow passengers all seemed at home in this environment. The women were waifish, impossibly glamorous models and socialites. The men were well-dressed playboys who practically reeked of old money. Everyone seemed to have stepped off the pages of *Vogue*. A crew member named Jason showed me to my room.

"Sunset is in an hour, we will have cocktails on the north deck."

THE NEXT FEW DAYS WERE UNBELIEVABLE. It was like being air-dropped into an episode of *Lifestyles of the Rich and Famous*. At no point in my middle-class upbringing, no matter how much I fantasized about the kind of life I wanted, had I envisioned the degree of luxury that real money could buy. Reardon, Phillip, and I spent the next few days lazing in the sun on deck and eating sumptuous meals prepared by the boat's chef. At night, we went to parties on other boats, or headed into South Beach to dance at the clubs, where we were always ushered to the front of the line and treated like royalty.

The clubs also blew my mind. All the clichés of wealth and excess were in full effect in these places. A group of famous models was snorting cocaine off their compacts with hundred-dollar bills. Bottle after bottle of champagne was poured or sprayed . . . I lost count after fifty bottles, which meant that there was $50,000 worth of Dom and Cristal on the floor. Another model was making out with the handsome Greek shipping heir who had become visible due to a high profile relationship with Paris Hilton. A few seconds later, Paris walked into the club and beelined for her ex and his new friend. My eyes flew open as the pretty blond socialite punched the other girl right in the face. I seemed to be the only one noticing the commotion.

No one seemed to care about anything but having fun. There were no rules, no limitations, and no concern for the monstrous bar tab, which

I calculated must have been at least $80,000–$100,000 on champagne alone. The models attracted wealthy men, professional athletes, and celebrities. Each night at the club, I tried to overcome my shyness and talk to as many people as possible, casually mentioning poker and collecting names. These lawless playgrounds for the rich and famous were the ultimate fertile ground for finding new players. I was always working that angle. It was amazing how many numbers I got, either from potential players themselves or from someone who knew someone that loved to play. Poker easily broke down walls.

On New Year's Eve, we went to a party hosted by P. Diddy. Some of the biggest names in music took turns performing. Someone passed me an Ecstasy pill. I had always been afraid of drugs, but I popped it in my mouth. Thirty minutes later I felt like every cell in my body was tingling and I was in a soft bubble of happiness and love. The music, the lights, everything was beautiful and perfect. All I wanted to do was dance. Everyone was my best friend and when midnight came glitter filled the air, and it seemed like everyone in the world wanted to kiss me. We shouted the countdown and I couldn't remember any other time in my life when I had been happier.

AFTER THE AFTER-PARTY and the after-after-party, the first signs of dawn sent the partygoers fleeing for bed like vampires. My pill had worn off for the most part, but I still felt fuzzy and content.

"Oh my God, I seriously can't watch the sun come up again," I overheard a leggy brunette exclaim, leaving a trail of sequins behind her.

"I know, it totallllyyy freaks me out," said her blond friend, looking the worse for wear.

"Let's take our Xanax now," she said, and in unison they popped open matching pill bottles and swallowed the little white pills without anything to drink. When I got back to the boat, I was starving, so I went to the kitchen to fix myself a snack. My ears were still ringing from the loud music in the club and I felt too full of adrenaline to sleep. I grabbed my food and climbed to the very top of the ship. My mind started to return to reality. I sat cross-legged and watched as the sun came up over the ocean. Tomorrow we were going back to L.A. and everything would be different. I had been so high off my victory, and over the fact that my relationship with Reardon had survived my scheme, that I didn't even think about what taking over the game really meant. I had been under Reardon's protective, if not oppressive, umbrella. Now it was just me. No fall guy, no crazy lunatic that scared everyone standing behind me. I knew I had a lot to learn, and not a lot of time to study. But somehow I wasn't scared. I was excited. Anything could happen, and my fate was finally all up to me.

Chapter 14

I returned from Miami filled with energy, my brain flooded with ideas I wanted to implement in the game.

My dad was someone who was always processing and analyzing everything. Discussions were never simple with him, words were dissected, references sourced. Growing up with this was sometimes annoying, but I realized what an important skill this kind of thinking actually was in the real world. In order to really run the game the way I dreamed, to offer value and to make myself irreplaceable, I needed to process and analyze my players. I needed to get inside the psyche of the gambler.

I was aware that this was not a traditional game of poker. The stakes were too high to make it a friendly at-home game, complete with nachos and beer. The players weren't pros, and they were too rich to be playing for a living.

My game was about escapism. In order to offer complete escape, I had to offer more than just chips, cards, and a table. I had to sell a dream—a dream of an even better, more exciting life in which the recruit could hobnob with celebrities, beautiful women, and be catered to like he was the most important person at the table.

For the person to be willing to escape into the world of poker, however, he had to have the gene. These players could afford to escape anywhere in the world. I needed them to escape at my table, not in Maui or Aspen.

They needed to want to play poker. In a regular setting you could never detect who had the gene. Net worth had nothing to do with it; nor did social class, ethnicity, or career path. This was part of what made the table so interesting—here was an eclectic group, brought together by some sort of genetic mutation. And, for all the negative stigmas, gamblers seem to have an endless reserve of hope and optimism. They all believe they can make something out of nothing. They would show up with renewed hope each week, regardless of the results or outcomes of weeks past. Especially if along with the thrill of the fight came an assistant who handled every aspect of the game and any aspect of their lives if they wanted. That assistant, of course, was me.

So, my assets were an ability to provide escape, a nose for sniffing out those with the gene, creating an environment where the excitement of the win could be fostered, and myself.

Lesson one: make sure your players are always comfortable.

Lesson two: feed the machine new blood.

Lesson three: be irreplaceable.

Lesson four: it's always about the money. I had clearly learned a lot from my father.

I WENT TO WORK IMMEDIATELY.

I set up appointments at the three most luxurious hotels in Los Angeles.

My first stop was the Peninsula, a quietly elegant hotel that catered to the richest of the rich. I drove onto the cobblestone drive and met the hotel manager, who was polished down to his Prada loafers. After having his staff pull me a foamy cappuccino, he escorted me around the hotel so I could see the dreamy rooms and the manicured grounds.

By now, I had figured out how to operate with confidence, or fake it till I made it.

"I'm going to be hosting 'industry networking events,'" I explained to him. "There will be a lot of celebrities attending . . ." I paused for effect. Even at the ritziest addresses, the promise of certain high-placed attendees could always open doors. "So . . ."

I let the sentence hang.

"You understand the need for a certain level of privacy."

"Of course," he said. "Of course. Anything you need, Miss Bloom."

"I'll need a poker table delivered to the room on the day in question," I said. "You know how boys are!"

I laughed lightly and he laughed along with me, telling me that yes, he knew.

"We can certainly accommodate any need you may have," he assured me. "Let me give you my card. I've written my cell-phone number on it . . . Please don't hesitate to call should you need anything else."

He practically kissed me on the way out the door. And he wasn't the only one: my meetings at the Four Seasons and the Beverly Hills Hotel went much the same way. I told their managers the same story I had offered at the Peninsula, and threw in that I would be using the best room they had on a weekly basis. I was starting to realize what Phillip had meant during our lesson. Bluff and perception are much more important than actual truth and circumstance.

At every hotel I visited, I was offered the same royal reception. It was amazing the impact that celebrity had on everyone in this town. I felt like I could have told the staff that I was having an arms-dealing, drug-trafficking, and prostitution event that marquee names would be attending and they would have nodded, cooed, and accommodated.

I left the last meeting on a cloud. With three luxury locations on call, I could move the game around at my leisure, which would have three great benefits: the game would be less of a target for anyone trying to infiltrate; I would control the location; and it would be more mysterious, which I believed was always a positive, especially with gambling . . . and men.

Everything was going my way. All I could think was, *Let the games begin.*

BEING ON MY OWN WITHOUT REARDON meant that I needed to make sure this thing was legal, for real.

The players said their lawyers had all told them that the game was in the clear, but that wasn't sufficient to make me feel safe, or offer me any useful information specific to *my* role.

I needed my own lawyer.

Wendall Winklestein was a top criminal attorney who came highly recommended by several of the guys from the game. Wendall had a swanky office with expensive artwork on the walls. His taste was a visual testament to the fact that rich people often behaved badly.

I walked into his office and I felt him leering at me from behind his desk.

"So you're the little poker princess."

I frowned on the inside, but offered a weak laugh.

"I've been hosting poker games, yes," I said. "I want to make sure that it's legal."

He switched gears from lecher to lawyer.

"Are you taking a rake?"

"No," I said.

"How do you make money?"

"Tips."

He raised his eyebrows.

"Everyone wants to play in the game," I explained. "On the first night my former boss told the players they needed to tip me to be invited back."

Wendall laughed. "Smart."

Then he got serious again.

"Here's my biggest piece of advice," he said. "Don't break the law when you're breaking the law."

"What do you mean?"

"What you're doing is in what we call a 'gray area.' It does not violate state or federal statutes, but it's a bit undefined. You need to keep your nose clean. No drugs, no hookers, no booking sports bets or hiring muscle to collect debts, and Molly, pay your taxes."

"I can handle that," I said.

"If you want to hire me, I require a twenty-five-thousand-dollar retainer," said Winklestein. The way he looked at me, I wondered if he might have some other form of payment in mind.

"How about cash?" I asked. I pulled an envelope out of my bag, having been prepared for this amount.

"Cash works." He smiled lecherously.

I HELD MY FIRST GAME at the Peninsula hotel because my contact there had offered a sizeable discount on the room. The game was called for 8 P.M., but I requested early check-in so that I could make sure everything would be perfect.

Diego met me with the table, and the hotel manager greeted us with enthusiasm, calling for the bellman to help us put it in the service elevator and take it upstairs. Once the bellman had taken his tip and gone, Diego and I rearranged the furniture to make room for the centerpiece: the poker table with ten chairs and ten stacks of chips, and, of course, Tobey's Shuffle Master. Diego left with promises to return an hour before the game started, and then I was alone in this amazing, gorgeous, palatial suite.

I raced around checking everything out. The bathroom was nearly as big as my whole apartment, and it had those amazing fluffy robes that you see in movies. The manager had left me a bottle of champagne and a fruit plate. I opened the bottle and poured myself a glass. Even the berries tasted better in a place like this. I raced to the bed. It was heaven. I didn't realize a bed could be so comfortable. I threw myself into a pile of down pillows and giggled out loud.

The game wouldn't start for another six hours, so I changed into my bikini and headed for the pool. The rooftop pool at the Peninsula had a beautiful view of the city. It was decorated from the cabanas to the heavenly lounge chairs in all white, with only the turquoise pool and bright blue sky as accents. I settled into a soft chaise; the sun was warm and a cool breeze blew from the west. One of the pool boys walked by, spritzed me with rose water, and handed me two slices of cucumber to put over my eyes. He asked me for my room number and came back in a couple minutes with a Bellini, compliments of the hotel manager. I sipped my Bellini in my private cabana, feeling like life couldn't get any better. But if I wanted to hang on to all this, I had to stay sharp and work hard. I put down my drink and started fielding calls from the players.

IT WASN'T UNTIL I SAT DOWN to get ready that I returned to earth, and began to feel nervous about the game. I looked at my face, bare of makeup, free of pretense. Was I in over my head? Yes, since the day I drove into town, but that wasn't going to stop me.

Tonight's game was going to be a familiar group—Reardon, Steve Brill, Reardon's partner Cam, Tobey, Houston Curtis, Bob Safai, Bruce Parker, and Nick Cassavetes. As usual, I had given Tobey a heads-up on the lineup, the courtesy he demanded and that saved me from his terrifying death glare if he came in and found an unknown at the table.

"Fine," he had said. And that was when I sent the text to everyone else. Everybody I invited said yes.

I couldn't wait to see their faces when they walked into this gorgeous room and saw what their game was going to look like from now on. Everything was designed to be amazing. I had even hired two professional masseuses to give shoulder rubs, something a few of the guys had mentioned wanting. I vetted the women to make sure they were licensed; you just never know in Hollywood, especially when there are rich and famous people involved. I even had my attorney draft NDAs for them to sign.

The biggest danger was getting too busy and forgetting to write down a buy-in. The guys were supposed to sign for their buy-ins, but sometimes they were so grumpy they refused, or thought it was bad luck to sign their initials. I insisted so that after the game no one could contest the accounting. Now that I was in charge, I was going to have to be more assertive. One mistake meant the books would be off at least five thousand maybe more and I would be responsible to make up any difference. Two mistakes were . . . I couldn't even think about it.

In an effort to forestall any potential disasters, I had asked Diego to help me with the buy-ins and the books, and I had asked my friend Melissa to help me out with managing the guys' requests. She would be there to refill drinks and run out for the food order, which could cost thousands of dollars a night and was so extensive and detailed that obtaining it was almost a full-time job in itself.

THE SUITE WE HAD BEEN GIVEN was on one of the top floors, a stunning affair done in the whites, beiges, pale pinks, and golds of expensive furnishings. French doors opened to a wraparound patio. There was a table laden with fruit plates, cheese plates, charcuterie, and fine chocolates. A cool breeze was blowing in, freshening the room, which smelled of Dyptique candles and fresh-cut flowers. The two masseuses were on hand, Melissa had arrived on time, and Diego brought an additional dealer with him. There was music playing quietly. I was wearing a long white dress, lots of gold jewelry, and I had piled my long hair on top of my head.

The first to arrive was Houston Curtis (as always).

"Wow! This is great!" He walked out onto the patio to admire the view.

I joined him outside, and Melissa approached to offer him a drink.

"Can I get you anything? Water, tea, champagne?"

Houston, the man who always wanted diet raspberry Snapple (which I had chilling in the fridge), checked out his surroundings and upgraded his order.

"Champagne? Why not?"

I smiled.

"You like it? You think the other guys will like it?"

"Oh yeah! It's classy. It'll be nice to not be at Viper anymore. I mean, I loved the Viper. But this place just feels nice. It even smells good."

Reardon showed up next.

"Roguish, player," he said, wandering from room to room.

He checked his phone and shoved it in my face. The picture on the phone was of some young beautiful naked girls assuming a very flexible pose.

"Might need this room later," he said, laughing and grabbing for the menu. "Mol, order me some caviar. Ossetra, with toast points and—"

"I got it, Reardon," I said. "I know what you like."

We were both laughing now.

The rest of the guys showed up, all of them with expressions of approval at the shift in atmosphere.

Tobey arrived last.

"Nice!" he commented.

I looked at him in surprise; a nicety from Tobey was like a hug from the Queen.

As the men settled themselves around the table and Diego started to deal the cards, I sat in a chair at the side, taking the scene in like I was watching a film that I had directed. They shuffled the chips in their hands, creating a chorus of clicks that had become as familiar to me as the sound of street traffic. The chips pooled around the players, and made their way into stacks of varying heights. I watched them play and chat, leaning back in those chairs while pretty girls rubbed their shoulders and they forgot about everything in their lives but what was happening in this room, and I knew that I had succeeded. The entire cast was hitting their marks. I watched Melissa ferry cocktails, watched Diego's hands fly, watched Tobey watch the other players.

There was something about the rich atmosphere that drove the stakes higher. Barely three hours had passed before Bob Safai was down $300,000, a huge number for a game with a $5,000 buy-in. Steve Brill, somehow, was winning most of the money. I held my breath for a moment, but then I relaxed again, because Safai barely seemed to mind.

It was 4 A.M. before the last of them left, and as the door shut behind them, Diego high-fived me.

"Nice game. You did it. You won."

"*We* won," I said.

I counted the tips and divided the stacks. Ten thousand for each of us.

Chapter 15

The guys loved playing in the hotels. They loved the added amenities. Additionally, I trained my staff to say yes to everything unless is was illegal or demeaning. Instead of creating my own expensive backdrop, I took advantage of the fact that the premier hotels I had chosen had already thought of everything. They were already accustomed to the demands of the richest, most entitled guests (not saying that my guys were this, but the staff in a place like this was prepared for anything).

I started creating a poker kit, based on the requests I received most often. Single-malt scotch, caviar, champagne. You need a phone charger? Got it. You have a headache? Excedrin and a cold compress. Stomach hurts? Got that. You need travel reservations that can't go through your company? I just need the details. You need me to book a room at the Four Seasons for next week? No problem, what kind of room? Your girl has been dying for the sold-out "it" bag? I'll deduct it from your win and handle it. You need an acupuncturist, at the game, while you play—done. It was all yes all the time. I couldn't ignore that yes had become my mantra. I shared a name with the very famous literary character from James Joyce's epic novel *Ulysses*. Her final soliloquy is about saying yes to falling in love and surrendering to her husband. I was also falling in love. With a poker game.

THE UPGRADED LOCATION and the fact that every man was treated as if he were James Bond only made the game an even hotter ticket. I started making so much money that I barely knew what to do with it. I started to slowly upgrade my life. Reardon let me take over the lease on his S-class Mercedes. It was fast, sexy, silver, and sleek. I loved his car and I used to sit in the passenger seat as he dictated a hundred demands, cut everyone off on the road, and yelled at his cell phone. I used to try to block him out and imagine if this car were mine. It happened a lot sooner than I thought it would. He came over to my apartment to drop it off. He threw me the keys.

"Have fun with your new car, player," he said, smiling like a proud father . . . or a mad scientist maybe.

His new assistant (he'd had five in the three months since we had returned from Miami) looked scared and uncertain behind the wheel of the car she had driven, following Reardon to my house.

"MOVE OVER, WHAT ARE YOU STUPID?" he yelled at the young blond girl. She looked terrified and crawled awkwardly over the gearshift. I looked at Reardon with a disappointed frown. And then I smiled warmly at her.

"If you are half as good as Molly was, I may give you a car, but I highly doubt that. You've got a tough act to follow." I smiled on my face and in my heart. As flawed as Reardon was, I knew he loved me. He sped off in a cloud of dust, gravel, and insults.

"BLAIR!" I yelled. She came outside.

"Look at my new car!!" I said, jumping up and down. I had grown past the downplaying-everything phase.

"Wow! Are you serious? Let's go for a ride!"

I got in and slid the seat as far forward as it would go, sat up tall, and tried to put the key into the ignition. It wouldn't go in.

"Oh, my dad has a car like this. Put your foot on the brake and press that button. And lean your seat back a little. You look like you are driving for the first time." She laughed.

I did as I was told and the V-12 engine let out a smooth guttural purr. I stepped on the gas and we both screamed as it shot us up the hill at an alarming speed.

I turned left on Sunset and put down the windows and turned on the radio. Everyone on the street looked at us. Apparently a nice car in L.A. meant a hell of a lot. I stepped on the gas again and my sleek Mercedes barreled forward so fast I was thrown back into my plush seat. Blair laughed. "It's a lot of power for you. You sure you can handle it."

I smiled and didn't want to say what was in my mind because it was obnoxious. But power is what I wanted. I wanted more, I loved it. I floored the gas pedal. We were going ninety-five on Sunset.

I liked the thrill and the adrenaline rush that breaking the law gave me. I switched lanes and passed cars. I was drunk on the power under my foot. Suddenly I saw a cop behind me turning on his lights. I turned into the Beverly Hills Hotel with screeching wheels. The valets all knew me.

"Welcome back, Miss Bloom," they said.

We had lunch by the pool, expecting to see a police officer the whole time, but he never came.

I HAD LIVED WITH BLAIR in the apartment her parents had bought her for two years. It felt like a lifetime ago that we had met at some silly party, hiding in the bathroom from a scorned reality-TV star. Blair had a serious boyfriend now, and I was ready to leave the nest. I was ready for independence, an apartment of my own. My whole life I had lived with other people, and the prospect of a place of my own was really exciting. I found an apartment on the twentieth floor in a fancy building on Sunset. Every other time I had rented an apartment in the past had been a stressful situation of coming up with the money, asking my parents, trying to collect from my roommates, and always coming up short. I took one look at the view, the sexy marble-and-mirrored bathroom, and the ample bedroom, and I had to have it. The broker started adding up: first month, last, and security . . .

I turned to her and cut her off while she was pecking at her calculator.

"Tell the owner I'll pay the first six months up front, in cash, for a discount."

The older woman looked at me in surprise.

"Well then . . . all cash?"

"All cash."

I had heard Reardon do this type of negotiating a hundred times, but I had never had the money or opportunity to do it myself.

I held my breath expecting the broker, Sharon, with her buttoned-up cardigan and French twist to scoff at me and call the police. But instead she said, "Give me a moment." She returned with a smile and a less tight look on her face. "My client would be happy to work with you on the price," she said. I negotiated a great deal, all by myself. And although the rent was five times more than I had ever paid, this apartment was all mine. I decorated it with beautiful furniture, gorgeously soft linens, lush rugs, and even art.

THE GAME SEEMED UNSTOPPABLE, each night more epic than the last. My phone never stopped ringing. Slowly but surely I stopped talking to all my old friends. I was changing; I could feel it. I loved being in those hotel rooms, I loved the sounds, the smells. I had become secretive; if anyone ever asked me what I did, I lied. I said I was an event planner.

I had noticed the impact of presentation and I worked on mine. I bought expensive clothes and shoes. I hired a trainer, got facials, manicures, and pedicures, got my hair done at the best salons, and went back to Valerie's for the works. I barely recognized the girl in the mirror.

I also wanted to work on my mind. I took French lessons, studied art, and read books on business and strategy. I absorbed the knowledge thrown around at the table like a sponge. I became great at math, as I had numbers in my head all the time. I watched the guys play, watched them lie to each other, learned their strengths, weaknesses, and their tells.

Chapter 16

Reardon and I became best buds. I helped train his constant stream of new assistants (no one lasted more than a month), and he advised me on business. He was still crazy, but that was who he was and I grew to love his idiosyncrasies. He called me one afternoon while I was updating my spreadsheets by the pool.

"Coming to get you, be outside in five."

"Reardon, I can't. I'm not dressed and I'm in the middle of something."

"Just be outside, five." And he hung up. I ran upstairs and threw something over my suit and put my hair up in a quick ponytail. In some ways I would always think of him as my boss. I had no idea where we were headed. But I was standing outside as ordered, in five minutes.

He looked at me when I got into the car.

"You look different," he said.

"Different, how?" I asked

"Better." He grunted. "Not so much like a homeless girl from Colorado." Reardon loved to tell people he found me on the streets of Beverly Hills with a backpack and no home. He wasn't that far off, but it was his favorite story to exaggerate. I guess the slow process of my L.A. makeover was complete.

"Thanks, dick, and I wasn't homeless," I said

His phone rang, he answered, and the rest of the way, he was screaming on his phone and driving 100 mph, as usual. He whipped his car into valet at the Beverly Hills Hotel and strode purposefully down the red carpet. I practically had to run to keep up with him. We took our seats at the counter and Reardon slammed a stack of newspapers down on the chair next to him. I was used to this behavior. Even though it was just the two of us, he demanded a table for four—partially because he liked to order the whole menu and partially because he hated to be close to strangers and their germs, unless, of course, those strangers were naked women. He glanced over at me and smiled.

"McCourt's meeting us," he said. It was surprisingly sweet the way Reardon was trying to play matchmaker.

My stomach did a little belly flop and I kept my head down as I saw Drew approaching out of the corner of my eye. I pretended to be engrossed in the paper.

"Hi, Molly," he said warmly

"Hi, Drew." I grinned.

I hadn't seen him for quite a while, but I thought about him often. He was the only guy I had met in L.A. who made me think twice.

Drew and I talked throughout the whole meal while Reardon texted, e-mailed, ripped through the paper, and ran off every five minutes to make a call. It was so easy to talk to him. After the three of us finished lunch, Reardon shoved a wad of cash into my hand, saying, "Pay for this, I'll be back."

That was Reardon's way of saying, *I'm leaving you here. Fend for yourself.*

"So what are you up to this afternoon?" asked Drew.

"I was working until I got hijacked by that terrorist." I motioned to Reardon's disappearing figure. "Who may or may not be leaving me here with no ride."

I silently cursed Reardon for putting me in this awkward position with the only guy I had liked in a long time.

Drew laughed. "I'm going to stop by my friend's house. He lives next door. Want to come along?"

Of course I did.

A FEW WEEKS LATER, I was helping Reardon's new assistant, Jenna, prepare for a dinner party at Reardon's new house. Reardon wanted it to go off perfectly and had requested that I show Jenna the ropes. Jenna was a gorgeous brunette, not particularly smart, and for the record, had not been my first, second, or third choice among the interviewees. I had found skilled, professional women, and, of course, Reardon chose the one that looked like a lingerie model. By the way she fluttered her eyes and sashayed across the room, it was clear that she possessed a specific type of skill and knowledge, even if it had nothing to do with running an office.

Jenna was adept at getting what she wanted from men and women alike. She batted her huge brown eyes at me. "Thank Goddd you're helping me! You are saving my life. I have sooo much going on; it's crazyyy."

"Good stuff, I hope!" I said, knowing she was a struggling actress.

"I'm having an affair with a married man," she confessed. "And he's not treating me like a proper mistress."

That was not the response I was expecting.

"What do you mean?" I asked.

"He isn't paying enough attention to me, or taking care of my bills," she explained, her mouth in a full pout.

I winced.

"Well, you have a new job now, so you can pay them yourself!" I responded encouragingly.

"That's not the point," she whined. "I'm going to fix it, though."

"How?" I asked, horrified and intrigued at the same time.

"Well, he's a famous rock star, and I was in his music video. He said he and his wife are not getting along, and are probably headed for a divorce. They all say that, though." She tossed her head. "The last time he came over I made a video of us without him knowing. If he doesn't start treating me right, I'll release it!"

My eyes shot open wide. This was exactly the kind of assistant Reardon *didn't* need.

"That's so smart!" I said, keeping up my encouraging tone, as if we were best girlfriends. "Where did you hide the video?"

"In Reardon's guesthouse." She giggled. "That's where I made it!"

"Clever girl," I said, and sent her out on an errand. Then I went to find Reardon.

"I told you not to hire her," I said, indignant, hand on my hip.

"You have to fix this, I don't want this drama," Reardon said. "And fire her."

"REARDON!"

"Just fix it."

I still felt like I owed him, since he had let me have the game.

WHILE JENNA WAS OUT LOOKING for a brand of caviar that didn't exist, I went into the guesthouse and found the camera and the tape. I made another video of blank footage of the room and pocketed the blackmail tape.

I had a friend who used to tour with the band in question, and he put me in touch with Gage, star of music, and now, a sex tape.

Gage asked me to meet him at his studio, and when I got there, he was behind the glass singing. The whole situation was surreal. His manager greeted me with less enthusiasm than I would have expected, considering that I was saving his premier client from a world of hurt.

"How much?" he asked.

"What? Nothing!" I said, realizing that he thought I wanted to sell the tape.

"Really?"

"Yes, really," I said, offended.

"Really?" he asked.

"YES!" I said again.

"Gage, come here!"

Gage came out and gave me a sharp look.

"She doesn't want money," his manager said.

"Well, what DO you want?"

"Nothing, I just thought you would want it before it gets any airtime."

We walked to the back and they invited me to sit and chat for a bit.

"You want to come with us to Vegas for our show?" they asked.

I politely declined.

"Should we watch the video?" Gage asked devilishly.

"I have to get back to work," I lied.

"Thank you so much," Gage said. "How can I ever repay you?"

I thought about it for a minute. "Do you know anyone who plays poker?"

THE DINNER PARTY WAS CALLED for the following evening. Reardon's friends consisted of very wealthy degenerates and young, hot, decorative girls. It was actually nice to observe Reardon's life from this side.

Sam and Cam affectionately rubbed my head when they arrived.

"Look who's turned into a piece of ass," Cam yelled. (Cam didn't ever have an "inside" voice; yelling was his normal mode.)

I was waiting for someone specific, and Reardon knew it.

"Don't worry, he's coming," he said.

"Shut up, Reardon. I don't even know who you're talking about." I tried not to blush.

"What kind of trouble are you causing now, Green?" said a voice behind me. It was Drew. I spun around and he gave me a big hug.

"Hey, Molly," he said. "You look great!"

"Thanks, Drew," I said. I could feel myself blushing.

Cam gave Drew a big backslap.

"McCourt! What's happening, player. Your Dodgers crushed me this week. Lost a half mil on those fuckers. Needed a Brink's truck to pay my bookie, I'm not kidding, look."

He pulled out his phone and showed us a video of himself doing some weird dance in front of a Brink's truck.

"Look at the next video," he said. "It's me giving some girl the baker's dozen."

I did not need to see Cam giving any girl anything, let alone thirteen of anything.

"You want a drink?" I asked Drew.

"Sure." He laughed. "I'll come with you."

"I don't know how you do it," he said, still laughing as we walked away.

"I don't work in the office anymore," I explained. "Just the game. I'm just running the poker game now."

"What's going on with you?" I asked, trying to change the subject.

"I'm not with Shannen anymore."

"I'm sorry," I said, not meaning it.

"It's a good thing," he said.

I heard hooting and yelling outside, and looked out just in time to see Cam jump off Reardon's roof and into the pool.

"Oh, Jesus," I said. "This is getting off to an early start."

Drew and I spent most of the night together tucked into the corner of the couch, laughing at the crazy antics happening around us. It was so easy to talk to him. Hanging out with him felt both exciting and comfortable at the same time.

MY PHONE RANG A FEW DAYS LATER; it was Drew, wanting to know if I was free that evening.

"Dinner?" he asked.

"Sure," I said, feigning casual while inside my stomach was doing flip-flops.

"Pick you up?" he asked.

We went to Madeo's, ordered a bottle of wine, and talked about our families, current events, science, sports. We stayed until the waiters began closing the restaurant. He paid the bill and we walked outside, where a limo was waiting to drive me home.

I looked up at Drew, about to thank him for a wonderful evening, and he leaned in and kissed me. It was a perfect kiss.

The Hammer flashed the limo lights and honked, ruining the moment.

"Okay, bye," I said reluctantly, and got into the car.

"Is that your man, little shorty?" the Hammer asked.

I laughed. "Maybe, if you hadn't ruined the moment, the Hammer."

He chuckled.

"Don't give up the ass, little lady, make him work for it."

It wasn't every day you got advice at midnight from a convicted felon driving a stretch limo, but the Hammer was right. So, like a nice girl, I went home.

A WEEK LATER, I was following the directions Drew had given me to his family's house. Sunset to Holmby Hills, and then I slowed to make the hard left. There was a bodega on the side of the road offering maps to the stars' houses. The street widened and then the houses disappeared and there were only massive walls on either side crawling with ivy. All I could see was privacy walls and green, literally and figuratively.

I pulled up to the gate and pressed the call button. I was used to this routine now. Someone answered and I announced myself. The large gate swung open and I started up the driveway. I drove up the hill, and it just kept going and going. I looked around; the property must have been many acres because there were no other houses in sight. At the top of the driveway was a huge fountain surrounded by smaller fountains. The driveway was circular and the house itself, when I finally found it, was monstrous. I sat in the driveway taking deep breaths. I had seen fancy houses, but this was on another level: it was different when those fancy houses belonged to people who were my boyfriend's parents. Suddenly I was very self-conscious.

Get out of the car, Molly. They're just people. I stepped out gingerly, debating which entrance to approach.

Thankfully, at that moment Drew walked around the corner.

"Hi," he said.

"Hi," I said, keeping some distance between us.

"Do you wanna come in or you gonna just stay out here?" he asked. He then gave me a hug and I felt a little better.

I FOLLOWED DREW through the massive doors into a huge marble foyer. The ceiling must have been fifty feet high. The artwork on the wall was breathtaking, and the air smelled of fresh-cut flowers. We walked through a formal dining room that held the biggest table I had ever seen, and into the open kitchen, where Drew's mom was standing in front of the stove, cooking. Jamie was tiny, barely five three, pretty and blond. She put down her spatula and came over to me, extending her hand.

"I'm Molly," I said.

"Of course you are," Jamie said. Her eyes were kind and sincere. "I'm so happy to meet you."

The rest of the family trooped in. Drew's father, Frank, shook my hand genially. Frank was tall, and handsome; he and his wife made a fantastic-looking couple. Drew's three younger brothers, Travis, Casey, and Gavin, were all handsome and sweet.

"Can I help with anything?" I asked, remembering my manners.

"Oh no! But sit and chat me with me," Jamie said.

I perched at the bar in the kitchen and Frank and the boys sat in the other room, watching baseball highlights. Jamie and I had an instant connection. It felt so normal to be chatting with Drew's mom that it was easy to forget that we were in a thirty-thousand-square-foot mansion. While she diced, sliced, and simmered, she told me that not only was she the vice chairman of the Dodgers, she also had a law degree from Georgetown, a business degree from MIT, and had apparently gone to culinary school in Paris.

I helped Jamie carry the dishes to the table, and she called for the guys, who completely ignored her in a perfect approximation of every cliché about what guys were like when they were watching sports. So Jamie, all hundred and ten pounds of her, marched into the living room and laid down the law. They dutifully followed behind her and I watched her, in awe.

Dinner was better than good, it was mouthwatering, and easily one of the best meals I had enjoyed in L.A. The conversation ranged from sports, to politics, to business. They asked me about my family in Colorado and my event-planning business; I answered all their questions smoothly, telling myself that I wasn't really lying. I really did run my own business . . .

The night was filled with laughter and a natural ease. As I watched Drew joke around with his brothers, I was overwhelmed. I knew that I had growing feelings for Drew, but tonight was the kicker. The lifestyle, combined with closeness and normalcy . . . how could I not be falling for him? Plus, I loved his family. Minus the trappings, they were just like my family, and exactly the kind of family I wanted for myself someday.

By the time we finished drinking the Brunello that Frank had selected from the wine cellar, it was late. The boys had already gone up to do their homework, and Drew and Frank were discussing business in the living room .

"Molly," Jamie said. "It's so nice to see Drew so happy; he really likes you."

I smiled back at her and said quietly, "I really like him, too."

The truth was I was falling in love, hard and fast.

Chapter 17

Going to baseball games with Drew's family was nothing like going to games with my brothers when I was a kid. When I was young, we sat in the nosebleed section in jeans and sneakers, ate junk food, and got rowdy with the crowd. With the McCourts, I was well groomed and civilized. There were no Dodger dogs or beers. The family was dressed to the nines, sitting next to the dugout and always entertaining someone important. It was a pretty serious affair. They had invested a lot of money, time, and passion in the team, so every game was a major event.

This night, I was sitting between Drew and former Dodger manager Tommy Lasorda, watching an L.A.–San Diego game. I was grateful to have Tommy there. He lightened the mood and sang songs to me in between hitters.

"Having fun, Molly?" asked Tommy.

"Oh yes!" I said with enthusiasm, and he nodded and then turned back to talk to Frank

I may have elevated my poker game from the basement to the penthouse, but the empire over which I ruled would always be too unsavory to trot out at dinner parties. Certainly, it was not fit for the company I kept during my outings with the McCourts. Even Drew didn't know the full extent of what I was up to. All he knew was that I was sometimes vague and busy when I should have been giving him my complete attention.

THE STADIUM WAS ON FIRE. We were all witness to one of those incredible baseball comebacks that has a whole crowd hyperventilating, the kind of game that the phrase "edge of their seats" was coined to describe. The Dodgers were battling back against the Padres, and suddenly notched two more runs. Nomar Garciaparra got up to bat, and at the exact moment when he swung and connected perfectly, sending the ball high into the stands for a game-tying two-run homer, I felt my phone buzz in my pocket. It was Tobey.

Ben is calling you now. I gave him your number, MAKE SURE HE PLAYS.

The crowd was on its feet. The McCourts were hugging me ecstatically. My phone started ringing.

Ugh, of course, this had to happen. How could I possibly leave at this moment?

I wiggled out of the mass celebration and gave Drew an "I'm sorry" look. He didn't look happy, but I had no choice. I had to take this call.

Ever since I had officially taken over the game, whenever Tobey called, I answered. In the beginning of my reign over the game, his attention was flattering. But as I acclimated to my new role, I had come to realize that the discussions that once made me feel smart and special were, for him, all about strategy. Like the trick with the Shuffle Master, the "generous" loaner that had probably netted him $40,000 in profit over the last couple of years.

His latest push was to increase the stakes. This particular lobby was in my best interest as well, because my tips were based on a percentage of the winnings. While the percentage varied from player to player, bigger wins generally equaled bigger tips. The game I had been running had a $10,000 buy-in, but Tobey wanted to increase it to $50,000. I knew we would lose some crucial players if we went with the increase, so I wanted to make sure we had replacements ready before we made the change. I put the word out, and got leads on some players who were huge gamblers. I was in pursuit of Rick Salomon, a sizable player, and Arthur Grossman, the ultimate whale. I had also heard that Ben Affleck used to play, and play huge. I asked Tobey about him a couple times and Tobey had promised to reach out.

Now here was the call, and I had to answer, even though it was the bottom of the ninth and the Dodgers were battling for a win in a crucial game.

I ran far back into the tunnel, but the noise was still deafening. I picked up the phone and prayed things wouldn't be as loud on his end.

"Hello?"

"Hi, Molly," said a voice that was familiar to me from a dozen films. "It's Ben. Is this a bad time?"

"Not at all," I lied.

"I hear you've got quite the game."

"Yep. It's a great game, tons of action. Best part is that most people don't really know how to play."

Ben laughed heartily.

"Sounds fun. What's the buy-in?"

I paused. Fifty thousand was such a huge number, and I didn't want to scare him away. Celebrities were such a huge draw.

"I have a couple different games," I said. "The buy-in ranges from ten to fifty K."

"Great," he said. "I would probably be interested in the big game. The fifty K."

Standing with my back against the wall, listening to the crowd roar in the distance, I watched people pass by in a blur.

He was interested in a big game. Tobey had been right. The field was changing now, and the stakes were getting higher. I felt a surge of adrenaline. I had spent two years watching the kind of numbers a guy could lose in the $10,000 buy-in: six figures, easy. This game would be five times bigger. I was starting to understand how this world worked, to get a feel for it. Gambling is compulsive, and gamblers continually want to raise the stakes. I could have played it safe, kept the buy-in at $10,000, but playing it safe wasn't as much fun.

I returned to my seat. The Dodgers had miraculously clinched the win.

"Where were you?" Drew asked.

"Work stuff," I said

"It couldn't have waited?" he asked.

Although Drew knew about the game, it was hard to explain how it worked.

I could feel his disappointment but I stared straight ahead, hoping the moment would just pass. This was the first of many times when I would feel torn between my public life and my secret, underground one.

Chapter 18

*D*rew and I were going on a last-minute jaunt to Vegas, and I had promised him that for the next few days all of my attention would be on him. Realistically, however, there was no way I could go to Vegas without picking up a few leads, and this dimmed both my excitement about my upcoming romantic interlude and my potential networking possibilities.

The guys were playing twice a week now, on Tuesday and Thursday. That meant that I had Friday night, Saturday, and Sunday to hang out in Vegas, and Monday to come back and make sure that everything was copacetic for the week's tables.

Drew was going to arrive in thirty minutes, and I was rushing around my apartment trying to pack. I had just finished collections and payments from last night's game, and my housekeeper, who was staying with my dog, Lucy, for the weekend, was trying to help me get ready.

Drew called from downstairs just as I finished throwing dresses and jewelry and twenty grand in cash for a little gambling at the tables into my LV tote.

"You ready, babe?" he said.

"Two seconds!" I yelled, grabbing for my passport.

"Real two seconds or two seconds times ten minutes?" he teased.

"Real two seconds," I said. "Don't worry, I won't make Neil wait."

THE PLAN WAS TO FLY with Neil Jenkins, Drew's very wealthy, young, handsome friend; the kind of guy who only dated Victoria's Secret models, Playmates, and actresses. The kind of guy who had his own plane. I really liked Neil. He was handsome, charming, and an expert at having the most fun possible.

We met Neil at the private airport, where he was waiting with his entourage, which included four of the prettiest girls I had ever seen. The girls all knew each other, and once we were on board, they sat in the back, congregating on the couch and eyeing me coldly. I had never understood the dynamic of girls automatically hating other girls. I took the lead.

"Hi," I said. "My name is Molly and you are the prettiest girls I've ever seen. It's seriously intimidating."

They softened instantly, and midway through the forty-five-minute flight we were laughing and talking like we had known each other for a million years. Two darkly tinted Navigators were waiting at the airport to take us to the hotel, where we were ushered in via the VIP entrance. Our "room" was more like a mansion, with an astonishingly dramatic view of the city.

We stood together, looking out over the Strip, all of the hotels lit up like a Technicolor dream.

"I'm glad we're here," said Drew.

"Me too," I said. We needed a trip like this. I told myself to forget about work; that for the next few days, it really would be all about me and Drew. I wasn't here to work. I wasn't going to work. I wasn't even going to think about work.

Even though we were in Vegas, where gambling was king . . .

WHILE DREW WENT DOWN TO MEET NEIL, I got ready with my new girlfriends in the huge marble bathroom in their villa, which was even bigger than mine. Tiffany, Lauren, and Penelope made quite a trio. They were all Playmates, and when we walked into the casino I felt the power of this much beauty. Every single guy looked up from their tables to check us out.

It instantly dawned on me that this would be an incredibly effective way to recruit. My mind started racing. I liked these girls a lot, and we were having a great time, but I needed to figure out if I could trust them before I brought them into my world.

We found Neil and Drew in the high-stakes room at the blackjack table. The girls stood to the side.

"Can I play?" I asked Drew and Neil.

"Sure!" they exclaimed.

Neil introduced me to his casino host.

"Blake," he said, "this is Molly. She runs the biggest poker games in L.A."

Blake straightened up and shook my hand solemnly. He gave me his business card and a "players' card," which would track my gambling play-time so the casinos could reward me with comps.

Drew and I settled in at the blackjack table. He was an adept player and I allowed him to advise me when I was unsure whether to hit or stand. In an hour and a half, I had turned $5,000 into $15,000.

"I'll be right back," I said.

I colored up, switching out the black hundred-dollar chips for a shorter stack of orange chips valued at one thousand each—and then went to talk to the host. I understood that he regularly "hosted" big gamblers like Neil, and his contacts could be very helpful to me.

I also knew that there was no such thing as favors, so I needed to incentivize him.

"Let's have a drink, Blake," I said.

"Sure," he said.

I glanced over at Drew, who was still happily playing cards. He barely seemed to be aware that I had slipped away.

I sat down at the bar next to the host and looked him in the eye.

"I think we can help each other," I said.

"How's that?" he asked, motioning to the bartender.

We ordered and I continued: "Well, I could always use new players for my game . . . and I've been thinking of organizing trips to Vegas. I could deliver ten huge players who would all use you as a host."

"Now, that's interesting," said Blake. The drinks arrived and he tilted his glass of Blue Label Johnnie Walker toward mine. "I think you just became my new best friend."

WHEN THE BOYS TIRED OF THE TABLES, we went out to the clubs. Drew and I sat together in a banquette while the girls danced around on the floor with Neil, attracting the eyes of every man there, including Rick Salomon, one of the players I'd had my eye on for some time. Rick was the videographer, director, and costar of the infamous Paris Hilton sex tape, which he sold to Vivid for a rumored $7 million. He was also reputed to be a huge gambler. We had met a couple of times, and I hadn't ever mentioned the game, but he knew who I was and I could tell he was a little wary (this wariness, I later realized, was full-blown paranoia). I sensed that I should wait for him to approach me.

The girls were slamming shots and dancing around provocatively—not only with each other but with the decorative but real naked girls who were covered only in gardenias—in a small bathtub on the stage. I saw Rick out of the corner of my eye, watching the spectacle.

"Hey, how's the game?" he asked me, his eyes glued to my new friends and the seductive performance onstage.

I gave him a look that clearly said that the game was insane, but I didn't speak. I wanted him to appreciate my commitment to discretion.

"Who plays?"

"I shouldn't say. I'm sure you know most of them."

He definitely did, he was a gambler, and this was the most iconic poker game in Los Angeles.

"Are they going to be there?" he asked, nodding toward my new friends.

"Yep," I lied.

"I'll call you when we get back to L.A. I'll probably play next week," he said.

He nodded at me again and walked away, while I smiled to myself at what could happen even when I was trying not to work. I had tripled my money at blackjack, and made a great connection with the host and with my new friends. I knew that all the Rick Salomons of the world were going to be easy prey.

I grabbed Drew's hand.

"You done being a politician?" He laughed.

"Yes!" I exclaimed and kissed him.

I poured myself a glass of champagne and was suddenly deliriously happy. That feeling swells inside your chest like a helium balloon. I closed my eyes and told myself to savor this moment.

Chapter 19

As soon as we got back from Vegas, I called Blake, the host from the hotel.

"I've got gold for you," he said. "I'm going to trust you that you'll come through with the trip."

"You have my word."

"His name is Derek Frost. He's young, rich, and a true degenerate. He's difficult, but he loses ten to twenty million a year. You want his number."

"What's his line of credit with you? How is he about settling his debts?"

"Three million. He always wants discounts and concessions but he always pays. He's a weird guy, though. Even though he is one of our biggest players, he prefers to fly Southwest, even though we would send any private plane he wanted."

I shook my head. Gamblers often had a unique perspective on money. At the beginning I didn't understand. I would shake my head in confusion as they complained about the price of the hotel room or the restaurants that catered the game, but had no problem betting six figures on a statistically dead hand. But I came to realize that every cent they bet represented an opportunity to make money, and even if the odds were against them, there was always a chance they could win.

I CALLED DEREK FROST, and we agreed to meet at a local coffee shop. When I arrived, the place was empty, which was strange for L.A. Nobody had office jobs here, and coffee shops were usually packed during the day.

I sat down outside in the sunshine and read through e-mails while I waited. After a few minutes, I looked up and saw a tall, darkly handsome man in—oh God—a *police officer's uniform* walking toward me.

"Molly?" he asked.

What the hell was going on here? Did Blake set me up? Was I getting arrested? I fought the urge to run.

"Yes," I said, nervous. "Are you Derek?"

I was trying to figure out if I could be committing any kind of crime by meeting a police officer for coffee in order to lure him to my "gray area" poker game.

"Don't worry," he said. "I'm just a volunteer cop. In my spare time."

"But that's still a cop, right?"

"Don't worry, we aren't after little girls and their games."

"You're not what I expected," I said.

"Likewise," he said. "I thought you would be older and not so cute."

I smiled, still totally thrown off and feeling like I needed to speak to my lawyer.

"Listen, if this were some attempt at a sting, would I show up here dressed in uniform?"

He had a point.

"Anyway," he continued, "it's a poker game, it's not illegal."

It was at moments like these that I realized I was walking a very fine line. In a truly legitimate line of work, one doesn't have a heart attack if a potential client shows up in law enforcement attire.

We went inside, where I learned a little bit about Derek. He hated Hollywood and the "fake people," and loved to gamble. He definitely wanted to play in the next game, and he definitely wanted to play in the big game.

"New players need to post," I said. "I can't extend any credit the first night. So anything you want to play with you have to bring, in cash."

"What about casino chips?"

"I'll take chips from Bellagio or Wynn," I said. Those were the only chips the other guys would accept as payment. I supposed this had to do with the fact that Steve Wynn was conservative and his casinos were solid. His stock was steady and he was a hands-on operator. My big guns knew the chips from his shops were good.

"No problem," he said.

"Oh, and Derek," I said. "May I suggest wearing civilian clothes?"

He laughed.

"You got it."

WITH THE ADDITION OF BEN, Derek, and Rick, I had more than enough players for the big game, and I started planning for the following Tuesday at the Beverly Hills Hotel. I asked for Bungalow number one because it was separate from the hotel, impressively appointed, and had a circular foyer that would be useful for keeping the food deliveries and room service separate from the game.

More celebrities and higher stakes meant that ensuring privacy was becoming more and more important. The higher the stakes, the greater the paranoia.

There were a lot of variables with this big game, and I was both nervous and excited. How would Rick mesh with the more civilized players? How much money would Derek bring? Would Ben like the game? I decided to drop Ben's name in an effort to land Arthur Grossman.

I had been doing some checking around about Arthur, who was known for his love of women and his mysterious but ample fortune. I knew that Arthur had more than enough billions to cover his buy-in. I also knew that he loved celebrity, and that Ben Affleck was a perfect line to dangle.

Hey, Arthur, I'm doing a game for Ben and we would love it if you played, I texted him.

It wasn't a total lie: I was doing a game, Ben was playing, and there were certainly a lot of players who would love it if Arthur played. Changing the phrasing around just made it seem a little more enticing.

Then I called Tobey.

"Yo," he answered.

"Hi, you should call Arthur. I told him Ben was playing. I also have that new guy, Derek, and Rick said he's playing. If Arthur plays, this will be an insane lineup."

"Okay, I'll give him a jingle," Tobey said.

I laughed. An evil genius with a fondness for words like "jingle" and "bummer" was an evil genius I could appreciate.

Twenty minutes later Tobey called me back.

"He's in," he said.

"Nice work, Hannibal." I had taken to calling him Hannibal Lecter after a recent game. That evening, I watched as he talked a guy into folding a winning hand, also known as "folding the nuts" in poker terms.

"I swear on my mother's life I have you beat," he had said, convincingly and earnestly. "I wouldn't lie to you, man."

His opponent had gotten confused. I had watched him stare at the cards he was holding, knowing full well he had the winning hand but suddenly unsure after Tobey's performance. Tobey was incredibly convincing, and so earnest that the guy eventually, although reluctantly, gave in.

To add insult to injury, Tobey then victoriously showed his bluff. To me, his actions were in really bad taste.

"See you Tuesday."

Word was out now about the big game, and I had received a few calls from professional poker players practically begging me for a seat. Some offered me straight cash, and some a "free roll," which means if they won I would get a percentage and if they lost I wouldn't have any liability. I knew that letting pros into this game would be a surefire way to lose it. The pros would win all the money, and part of what made my game so special was the chemistry at the table and the fact that nobody there played poker for a living.

The final list for the big game was Tobey; Ben; my new whales, Derek Frost, Rick Salomon, and hopefully Arthur Grossman; Bob Safai; Houston Curtis; and some new faces—Bosko, a dapper gentleman in his sixties; Baxter, a finance whiz who loved to gamble; and Gabe Kaplan, who back in the day was the star of *Welcome Back, Kotter*. All the players except Tobey and Houston were huge action. The going-all-in, blind kind of action. And the initial buy-in was $50,000, which meant there would be half a million dollars on the table before the first cards were dealt. It was going to be a big night.

DIEGO MET ME AT THE HOTEL with the table. The bellman had rearranged the room according to my instructions.

Diego and I shared a special bond now. We were full-fledged partners in this strange and wonderful world.

I chose my outfit carefully that night: a black dress that was just clingy enough to be sexy but not enough to be vulgar. Black Louboutins, Chanel pearls, and a light jacket, which was important because I liked to keep the game room cool. Colder temperatures keep players awake, and there was nothing worse than a tableful of tired, lethargic poker players. I wanted the table exploding with action, energy, and conversation.

The chemistry at a table is so important. You must start with a carefully balanced mix of personalities. If the balance is off and the stakes are too big for some of the players, it kills the game. Too small, and everybody gets bored. The $50,000 buy-in had attracted these guys and so I knew they could handle it; I also knew that it would create pots big enough to make even the richest guys sweat a little.

I reapplied my lipstick and I waited. I had invited the new friends I had made in Vegas, the "playmates" Tiffany and Lauren. The two of them showed up to serve drinks and to serve as decoration. They looked breathtaking. I knew the guys in the room tonight would have a lot that made them want to stay—on and off the table.

The first player to arrive was Derek Frost, thankfully in regular clothes.

"Nice setup," he said, looking around the room and landing his gaze on Tiffany and Lauren. The two girls and I sat and chatted with Derek while we waited for the rest of the players to show. Tiffany was a real pro. She gazed at him with her turquoise-blue eyes, acted as if she were hanging on every word he uttered, laughed at his jokes, and made him feel like he was the one and only man in the world. It was impressive. And effective.

Maybe because he was so disarmed by Tiffany, or maybe because it was what everyone who doesn't have access says, Derek Frost, the guy who had bent my ear for an hour about how much he hated Hollywood and the scene, sure looked excited when Tobey showed up with Houston. I introduced them, and Tobey played his part of charming, funny movie star perfectly.

Baxter showed next. He was a very successful trader who seemed a little ditzy but was a genius with numbers. I'd heard he'd been banned from several casinos in his younger years for card counting and was an absolute animal at the table, as I found most traders were. He always had the same routine of arriving and emptying out his pockets, which always contained a shocking amount of items: golf tees, pens, receipts, lip balm. He handed me his blank, signed check and I clipped it to my board. Every player that night had done the same—given me a signed check, with the amount left blank to cover their buy-in, and their losses if things didn't go their way. For the moment the holding company of Molly Bloom Inc. was officially rich.

Baxter went to join the other guys and I motioned Derek over.

He picked up his backpack and followed me into the bedroom, opening the bag as soon as I shut the door. He knew what I wanted: he had $250,000 in cash and another $500,000 in Bellagio chips. As I explained to him at the coffee shop, I couldn't extend him credit, so by bringing $750,000 he would be able to buy in fifteen times that night.

Even though I was tripping on the amount of money I was being given, I smiled as if I did this every day. I didn't want Derek to start to wonder about the fact that he had just handed three-quarters of a million dollars to a virtual stranger. "Great, I'll just put it in the safe for now."

"Don't run off with it," he said.

"I won't, Officer Frost," I returned, winking.

We rejoined the others just in time to see Bosko and Gabe Kaplan walk in. They gave me a cool hello; they were old school and I knew it would take some time before they would show me any respect. I didn't care. My game spoke for itself.

Bob showed up next, and Baxter asked me if we could begin.

"Guys, do you want to start?" I asked, above the excited banter.

Of course they did.

THEY DREW FOR SEATS, and the game was off and running.

In the very first hand, Bob, Bosko, Baxter, and Derek were all in. I got the chips and the buy-in board ready. That hand went to Bob, which made both Bob and Diego, whom Bob punished when he lost, very happy.

The guys reloaded, laughing and joking.

"I'll take two hundred," said Baxter.

I looked around the room for objections. Baxter wanted to make sure he had enough chips to take Bob down.

"Actually," Baxter said, "make it five hundred."

I looked at him and he nodded, so I counted $500,000 in chips, and gave them to him.

"I'll take five hundred too," said Derek.

I looked at Tobey at the same moment as he looked at me, and nodded to indicate that I had the money in cash. His eyebrows flew up and he looked impressed.

I counted out Derek's chips.

"Give me three hundred more," Bob said.

Talk about a testosterone contest, I thought, counting out the chips. The cards hadn't even been dealt for the second hand. As I counted the chips I looked around the table to see if anyone else wanted to play Richest Guy at the Poker Table. With no takers, the action continued.

Eventually, Bosko and Gabe got up and went outside to smoke a cigar.

I was in the kitchen filling drink orders. I could hear the men's voices echoing from the patio.

"Who the hell is running this game?" Gabe asked. He sounded concerned. He had a lot of money on the table.

"The girl," said Bosko.

"The girl? What does she know? Who handles the money? Who extends credit? How do we know that Derek guy is good for it?"

"We need to have this conversation with Tobey," said Bosko. "We can't trust that girl to do this."

My balloon of happiness deflated. I wanted to stomp out there and tell them both that I was smart and capable and I was managing the details of this game to a degree that would make their HEADS SPIN.

But I didn't. I couldn't let them know they had gotten to me. This was no place for hurt feelings. I didn't need these guys to like me, but I needed them to trust that I knew what I was doing. I texted Tobey and asked him to go calm their nerves and get them back to the table.

Just then I got a text from Ben.

Here, it said.

A surge of excitement coursed through my body—and in that moment I realized how much I had changed. Back when I was a normal girl, the butterflies I'd be feeling at a moment like this would be because I was about to meet one of the most handsome, influential stars in the world. Ben Affleck showing up for my poker game was undeniably monumental, but the butterflies I was feeling now were excitement that he was playing at my table, that he was a part of my game.

I GREETED BEN AT THE DOOR. He was tall and handsome, with a relaxed charisma that not all icons have in person.

He looked surprised when I told him who I was.

"You're so young," he said.

"Not that young." I winked. I was twenty-seven but I looked even younger.

I took his coat and showed him the buy-in sheet.

His eyes flew open and he looked at his watch.

"Two million on the table already?"

"Yep," I said.

"Okay, give me fifty K."

By now I had learned something about the psychology behind the way a guy asks for chips. Wanting to be overstocked or short-stacked at a table is a clear indication of playing style and ego. Whereas some guys want the tallest piles they can manage, the better to bully the table and scare people, Ben's buy-in choice told me that he was a smart player who liked to limit his downside, especially at a table with a bunch of guys he wasn't used to playing with.

Rick Salomon showed up next. Rick was hot. He was crass and dirty, but he was still hot in a caveman kind of way.

I pulled him aside to show him the board.

"Wow, they are swingin', huh?" he said, looking down at me. "Wanna fuck?"

I looked back at him, praying my face wasn't as red as it felt.

"No thanks," I said, as casually as if he had asked me if I wanted a Tic Tac. He laughed.

"Give me two hundred K."

Holy shit. I had a HUMONGOUS poker game.

As Rick took a seat, I saw him focus on Ben. I saw the wheels turning. Oh God, I thought, don't let him say anything embarrassing. Rick had no filter.

"Hey, yo, did that Jennifer Lopez's ass have cellulite on it, or was it nice?"

The table went silent.

Ben looked at Rick.

"It was nice," he said, and pushed into a huge pot.

The table laughed and the ice was broken. These may have been larger-than-life characters playing with larger-than-life numbers, but at the end of the day, guys are guys—and strangers quickly became familiar friends at a poker table.

After that uncomfortable moment, and after Tobey assured Bosko and Gabe that I in fact knew what I was doing, the game took on a life of its own. It was one of those perfect nights where the conversation was lively, the action was fast and furious, and each one of my usually impossible-to-please players had a look on his face that said that he would rather be there, at this table, than anywhere in the world. My tips that night reflected the enormous success of the game. I think I walked away with close to $50,000. After the last player had left and Diego and I had cleaned up, I sat on the patio watching the sun come up. I had discovered an incredible niche, and I had learned the formula to make it successful and keep it legal. As long as I didn't take a rake, or a percentage of every pot, I wasn't breaking any laws. I didn't need to take a rake, as long as I kept the membership exclusive and limited to celebs, billionaires, and easy money, the players would pay through generous tipping in order to be invited back, to have admission into this exclusive club. I had found a loophole in the system; no one else was doing what I was doing. There were home games, raked games, and casino games; but no one had figured out how to create an environment so compelling and alluring and potentially lucrative that the tips the players left were actually an insurance policy that they would be invited back. I was paying taxes, I was playing by the rules, but I had made the rules work in my favor.

Part Four
COOLER

Los Angeles, 2008–2009

Cooler (noun)

A case in which playing a strong hand that normally justifies the maximum bet is beaten by a still stronger hand.

Chapter 20

*M*y games weren't the only thing that was going well. My summer with Drew had been a fairy tale. His parents had bought a house on Carbon Beach, the most expensive stretch of sand in Malibu, known as "Billionaires' Beach," and inhabited by celebrities and tycoons. They had also purchased the house next door, which at some point they planned to tear down in order to enlarge their home, but for that summer they gave it to Drew. We spent the weekends at the charming, multimillion-dollar beach shack.

The McCourts, despite their wealth and status, valued family time. Drew and I attended Sunday-night dinners and baseball games on a regular basis. I loved going to the Dodger games, and watching Drew's parents, Jamie and Frank, realize a lifelong dream of owning a sports team was both inspiring and romantic. We also spent a couple weeks in July at their Cape Cod summer home, and visited the Boston home where Drew had grown up. I wanted that summer to last forever, but it was quickly coming to a close.

It was the last weekend in August and Drew and I were enjoying a late-afternoon stroll along the beach. Lucy ran ahead barking at the waves and rolling in every disgusting smell she could find.

"What are we going to do for your birthday?" I asked. Drew's birthday was the second week in September.

"We could go to New York," he said. "Watch the finals of the U.S. Open, eat good food, and go to the Dodgers-Mets game."

I smiled. In my new world, summer vacation really never ended. It was always warm and sunny and there was always something new and exciting to plan.

"We can fly with my parents on their plane."

I wondered if I would ever get used to my new reality. I didn't want to. I always wanted to feel this excited, alive, this fortunate, this on fire. Halfway down the beach, hand in hand, we ran into Rick Salomon, who had rented a house on the beach for the summer, a stunning testament to the enormous profit porn could yield.

Shannen Doherty was Rick's ex-wife and Drew's ex-girlfriend, so I cringed a little, expecting an awkward encounter between the men, but neither of them seemed to care.

"Hey, you think we can get a poker game going tonight?" Rick asked.

"Sure," I said immediately.

"You should play, McCourt," Rick said.

"Another time," Drew said. I knew he would never do this, and that was one of the things I liked about him. He wasn't flashy and he seemed to have a healthy respect for the value of a dollar despite his family's wealth.

"I'll put out some feelers and call you in a few," I said.

As we walked back I turned to Drew.

"You don't care, right?"

I knew we had plans, but Drew would understand. It was business.

He said he didn't, but I felt some tension. It was work, and I would never stand in the way of his ambitions. Still I had a nagging feeling that I should have run it by him before I made plans to spend the night at the poker table, instead of at home with him.

I pulled the game together in an hour or so. There were many more spectators than usual that night, mostly girls in tiny bikinis. The rapper Nelly had somehow appeared. He was very polite, and his entourage sat quietly on the couches nearby. Since it was the last weekend of summer, there were many parties going on along the beach and various people wandered in. This wasn't how I usually ran things, but it was Rick's game. Just as I was giving Nelly another buy-in, Neils Kantor rushed in. He came from a very rich family that was well known for its important collections of modern art, and Neils possessed the exuberance of a child, but beneath the juvenile facade he had a shrewd business mind. He was motioning enthusiastically for me to come outside. I asked Diego to watch the game for me.

Neils grabbed my arm dramatically.

"You will thank me for this," he said, his eyes twinkling and his voice animated as he practically pulled me down the stairs onto the wet sand.

"I've known Brad for years, he runs a huge fund, and he does VERY WELL. Lots of people I know have invested millions with him. Brad is also a huge gambler. I ran into him on the beach and brought him to you."

Neils looked at me happily like a puppy that had retrieved a ball.

He was still pulling me when he stopped in front of an attractive guy dressed in beach clothes.

"This is Bradley Ruderman," Neils announced proudly.

Brad and I exchanged small talk and I invited him inside. Unfortunately I couldn't use Neils's endorsement as a guarantee. I didn't want to ask Neils to vogue either. "Voguing" means guaranteeing a loss for someone— in this case it meant that if Brad lost, Neils would cover the amount if Brad couldn't or didn't pay. The only vogue I really trusted was that of someone who played in the game, and Neils had not. He had the best intentions, I was sure, but I was in a difficult, and somewhat awkward, spot. I explained this all to Brad, who was now watching the game with a look in his eyes I had come to recognize as true degeneracy.

"I would love to let you play but I need you to post or get someone from the game to guarantee you."

"Would Arthur suffice?" he asked.

Arthur looked up and quickly nodded. That's all I needed. I set Brad up with chips.

Brad was the worst poker player I had ever seen. It seemed as though it was his first time playing the game. He lost buy-in after buy-in, until almost everyone at the table was up and he was the financier. The players were looking at me in disbelief as the feeding frenzy ran its course. I texted Arthur throughout, verifying each buy-in and explaining the situation. Arthur seemed unfazed.

He can afford it, he wrote.

At the end of the night Brad was down high six figures on a $10,000 buy-in. Yet he seemed totally happy.

"Do you mind, my house is a couple doors down. I'll just grab a check," he requested politely.

"Of course not," I said.

He practically ran out the door. I was sure he wasn't coming back, but ten minutes later he showed up with a check for the full amount.

"Thanks so much!" he said, giving me a kiss on the cheek. "Do you think I could play in the next game?" he promptly asked hopefully.

"Sure, I'll call you," I said, trying to hide my confusion.

Something had to give. This just seemed too good to be true. There was no way the check would clear. But it did, instantly. And so began the era of Bad Brad.

DREW, TRAVIS, AND I were still half drunk as we drove to the private airport to meet their parents. We had made an early celebration for Drew's birthday and no night was mild with our friends. Popping gum in my mouth and keeping my sunglasses on, I focused on keeping my balance as I marched up the narrow steps to the sleek G-5. Drew and Travis were in far worse shape. Drew and I claimed the couch in the back, holding in our laughter. His two younger brothers were forced to sit in front with Jamie and Frank, their parents, who were, as usual, focused on business.

I had been to New York City a few times—a summer camp excursion to the Statue of Liberty and Empire State Building, an overnight stay in Queens on the limited ski-team budget before heading to the Olympic Training Center in Lake Placid, and a layover on my way to Greece. I was excited to really see the city now. I grabbed a coffee in an attempt to sober up. I didn't want to miss a second of this experience. We landed at the private airport in Teeterboro, New Jersey, where we were met with slick black SUVs. I stared out the window at the shooting verticality of midtown Manhattan. We pulled up to the Four Seasons, and uniformed doormen rushed to open the car doors, retrieve our bags, and lead us into the opulent lobby. It was as if being rich filtered out the inconveniences of life and left you with only the best parts.

I stepped into the marble lobby and felt transported. I had never seen such dramatic elegance. We were led around the corner to the check-in area, where the manager was waiting to greet the McCourts personally.

The room I was sharing with Drew turned out to be a whole suite on the fortieth floor. I walked over to the window. We were literally in the sky. New York City had a terrifying beauty. I couldn't wait to experience it.

That night, we all went to Milos for a family dinner with Tommy Lasorda, and then Drew, one of his little brothers, and I went out to a club. Drew knew the promoters there, so we were shown the full VIP treatment. We stayed out way too late, which barely left time for a nap before we woke up early for a marathon day of sporting events. First we headed to the stadium for the Mets-Dodgers game, where we nursed our hangovers with Bloody Marys and watched the crowds roar from our box seats. Then we got back in the SUVs and drove to Flushing Meadows for the finals of the U.S. Open. Our seats were on the court. We were so close that I could actually see the sweat flying off Andy Roddick's face. After a quick change at the Four Seasons, we met for dinner at Il Mulino, and then went to a different club to meet different friends. New York moved at a pace and on a scale that I couldn't even begin to comprehend, and that fascinated me.

The night of Drew's actual birthday I ordered a cake and champagne to be sent to the room. He blew out his candles, assuring me that he'd made a wish. I poured champagne for us and sat on his lap. I wanted to tell him that I loved him, and that he was my best friend. I wanted to talk about our future, ask him what he wanted out of life, but such discussions just weren't Drew's style. He was so closed and guarded about his feelings. Our relationship depended on a certain amount of disconnection. But that night, I felt everything we didn't say.

Chapter 21

I returned from New York refreshed and inspired. My first order of business was to pay a debt I owed Blake, the Vegas host, which was holding up my end of the bargain for introducing me to Derek. I needed to bring my guys to his town for a weekend.

The second order of business was to organize a tournament. This was something my players had mentioned a couple times. It seemed a good way to recruit more guys to the table.

After several conversations with Blake, I realized that setting up a game in Vegas was going to be a bit challenging. First, I had to find a weekend that worked for at least eight of the players. Among those players had to be guys who would hit the tables too—blackjack, roulette, or baccarat players. This was Blake's requirement. The casino only makes real money on games where it's the players against the house. In poker, the players play each other and the house takes a minimal fee (the rake). Then I had to establish lines of credit for all of the players before the casino would send the plane. All the guys wanted to negotiate comps (the perks and freebies granted by the casino) and discounts on potential losses before they would take out a line of credit. Being the middleman for all of this was a big job. In fact, it was a nightmare.

Next I had to make sure I had plenty of beautiful girls who could come along on the trip. Most of my friends were playmates who were used to getting paid up front for appearances. I tried to explain to them that the tips they would receive on this trip would exceed their day rate, but despite this, they wanted guarantees. Then I had to try to explain to each guy why he couldn't have the biggest villa and why some of them were going to have to (gasp) share one of the three-bedroom, five-thousand-square-foot villas with each other. Then I had to actually plan the game, get a table delivered, transport the chips and Shuffle Master, and coordinate dinners and nights out at clubs.

The tournament itself was even more complicated.

Tournaments are very different from cash games, mostly because there is a finite amount of chips. The buy-in was to be $50,000 with one add-on, which was an option to rebuy. I was hoping to have four tables of eight players, and $3.2 million in the prize pool; with cash tables set up for the guys who "busted out" of the tournament (ran out of money).

For my first tournament, I needed a space that would be private and high end, but visible enough that other wealthy clients would be able to see what was going on. I wasn't going to waste this opportunity to recruit, both in terms of filling the table and flaunting the game I had filled with the rich and fabulous.

I also made a little trip to the Commerce Casino outside of L.A., and let a couple of the floormen know that if they sent any players my way for the tournament, I would compensate them generously.

Buzz about the tournament, the Vegas trip with playmates, and Brad Ruderman, who continued to lose six and seven figures every game, spread as I had hoped. Fast and furious. So when Jamie Gold contacted me, I wasn't surprised. But I still laid on the charm.

I set up a meeting with him at one of the pool cabanas at the Four Seasons. I invited the playmates. I had done my research on Jamie. He had just won the World Series of Poker Main Event; his $12 million win was the largest sum in the history of the tournament. Usually, I wouldn't have considered allowing a World Series champion into the game, but Jamie was an anomaly.

I had spent the night before our meeting watching the footage of the game. It was clear that Jamie was no pro; he was simply running hot and playing fearlessly. I had seen it in my own game—a player getting so hot he couldn't lose no matter how terribly he actually played his cards.

There were three things I liked about Jamie: his freshly minted bank-roll, his reckless style of play, and what I anticipated would be an enormously inflated ego and a fever to prove he wasn't a one-hit wonder. New money and a nobody at a table of somebodies? He would chase this streak for as long as his bankroll would allow.

JAMIE WAS PALE AND THIN and wore thick glasses. I watched him walk across the pool from behind my shades, not acknowledging him until he was standing in front of me, blocking the sun.

"Molly?" he said,

"Jamie! Hi! I recognize you from television," I said, stroking his ego. I would have never said that to a true celebrity, but I knew it would make Jamie want to live up to my implied perception.

I introduced my friends to him, and it was clear that he was appreciating the scene he was witnessing immensely.

"Sit," I insisted, throwing on a cover-up and signaling to the waiter to bring Jamie a glass of champagne.

I complimented him for his performance at the World Series and then launched into an explanation of my regular game.

"The buy-in is fifty K. But guys get deep pretty quickly. And really, the sky's the limit in terms of how high the blinds can get."

"No problem. The bigger the better," Jamie said.

I smiled.

"I don't generally allow pros," I told him.

"Oh, I'm not a pro," he said. "I have a talent management company, and I'm a producer . . ."

He droned on about his supposed career endeavors, which I figured probably weren't that profitable since, if what I'd heard was true, he had borrowed the $10,000 to buy in to the World Series.

"Well, plenty of your peers play in the game," I said, and proceeded to list the celebs and notable mentions who sat at my table. "I'm not sure if I have a seat this week, but I'll work you in. I can't extend any credit the first game, so if you could post—"

"No problem at all," gushed Jamie. As if on cue, the girls got up to go to the restroom. I watched Jamie watch them.

We were sitting there laughing and talking when Derek Frost appeared, looking surly. Derek walked up to the cabana and handed me a huge check to cover the previous week's losses.

"I never win," he grumped. "If I don't win this week, I'm quitting and I'm not going to Vegas."

My Vegas trip was planned for the upcoming weekend, and if Derek bailed, it would dramatically impact the game. My Vegas contact wanted Derek there. I needed him too.

I introduced the men, but Derek already knew who Jamie was. The two began to talk shop until the girls returned; Derek's eyes lit up at the sight of them and he seemed to forget about the big check, Jamie Gold, and his bad luck.

Tobey called then, and I excused myself to answer the phone.

"I gave Kenneth Redding your number," he said. "He's going to be in Los Angeles and he wants to play."

"Who is he?"

"He's huge action. Great for the game. He runs a massive hedge fund in New York. He plays in the New York game."

"The New York game?"

"Yes, it's a monster. And they play a mixed game." A "mixed" game meant not just Texas Hold'em, which was the style of poker at my games, but other styles like stud.

"How much?"

"Two-hundred-and-fifty-K buy-in."

I raised my brows. That was five times bigger than my game.

"I'll look for his call," I said. My mind was racing. What if I could expand this thing? What if I could start a game in New York City? I needed to impress Kenneth.

THERE WAS A TON OF BUZZ about that week's game. Kenneth had a reputation as a huge gambler, and Jamie and Derek quickly signed on to play. The rest of the playing field had been selected carefully, and the only conservative players were, as usual, Tobey and Houston.

I even got a call from Joe Fucinello, an old-school gambler who used to play with Larry Flynt and fifty-year poker veteran Doyle Brunson. Joe told great stories about these legendary figures. Apparently, Flynt liked to play cards so much that he came to his own game right after surgery, on a hospital bed with an IV stuck in his arm. He had his personal nurse play his hands for him.

"Hey, Molly," grumbled Joe. "I heard Kenneth is playing, you have a seat tonight?"

"I don't, I'm so sorry." It was a mere two hours before the game was set to start.

Joe started yelling.

"Well, you better fucking find one. Who the fuck do you think you are? You're going to deny me a seat? I don't think you know who you are dealing with."

Joe was a little guy, but he was scary. He hung out in high-level circles, but he had a street edge and allegedly, a checkered past. He was also great to have at a table. So I thought fast.

"Joe, calm down. Just show up. We'll rotate if we have to."

"All right," he said, calming down immediately. "Four Seasons?"

"Yep, room 1204, seven P.M."

"See you then," he said, almost sheepishly.

I WAS ALWAYS A LITTLE NERVOUS when a new player debuted, and tonight I had three—Jamie Gold, Kenneth Redding, and Joe Fucinello. Jamie Gold, as I had expected, seemed like he was on a mission to prove that he belonged in the billionaire boys' club, and he was proving it by playing like he had the same bottomless bankroll as his opponents.

Joe Fucinello, Derek Frost, and Kenneth Redding were playing in the same style. They were going head-to-head, all in, every other second. By 10 P.M., both Derek and Jamie were already in for half a million. The action was unlike any I had ever seen. It was being driven by my new recruits, and I realized that the stakes would never be high enough for these guys. They would keep pushing the envelope, trying to feel that adrenaline. Win or lose. All they wanted was to feel alive.

My phone rang. As if the night wasn't amazing enough, on the line was a friend who was out with A-Rod and looking for a game. I invited them over, but I didn't let anyone know. It would be cool, I thought, to have A-Rod just casually show up.

I was right. When A-Rod appeared, tall, handsome, and very polite, the heads jerked up from the table. Men, no matter what age, ilk, or net worth, idolize a professional athlete. As they recognized him, they turned into excitable little boys. And as A-Rod took in the glamorous, well-appointed poker game I was running, a game that happened to have millions of dollars in chips on the table, the posturing started.

"If I win over three hundred K in this next orbit," Derek announced suddenly, "I'll give Bird five K, and twenty K to Polar Bear." Bird, one of my masseuses, was a struggling single mom. Polar Bear was the second dealer that Diego brought along. Now that the games were lasting longer and longer, the players wanted a dealer change because they thought Diego was bad luck.

Polar Bear didn't have two pennies to rub together, let alone twenty grand, and his eyes lit up. Unfortunately, Derek had his clock cleaned by Kenneth.

Kenneth was running all over the table, Joe was in for a million, and Jamie was about to be in for $850,000. Tobey was asking for a list of every vegan dessert in the city. And I was overextended, over my head, and loving every second of it.

Alex Rodriguez was watching it all, and having a great time.

"You're awesome, and your game is awesome," he said, on his way out. "You should come to Miami!"

"Call me," I said.

I had wanted to be more attentive to this incredibly famous baseball star, which would be a huge draw, but the game had spoken for itself.

And I was distracted by Derek, who loved to whine. He was texting me about his terrible, terrible luck, and how nothing good ever happened to him, how he had a permanent black cloud over his head. Except that his company netted him about $20 million a year. He loved getting passionately heated and launching into an hour-long diatribe about this injustice or that one, loved it so much I was starting to think that he liked to lose.

By the time the night was over, Kenneth had won a huge number, which was actually bad for my game. Since I had started keeping books, I had realized I had created an almost perfect balance. Despite the extraordinarily large results, the money essentially changed hands throughout the year. Most people were even or close to even. The exceptions were Tobey, Houston, Diego, and me. We were all big winners. And Brad was a loser.

But here was Kenneth taking $1.4 million out of my game and bringing it back to New York City. The only good thing about his winning was that he loved my game. I had made a good impression indeed. I had to make sure to keep in touch with him, I told myself. I was intrigued by this mythical New York City game. I wanted to know more.

Meanwhile, the game at hand beckoned. Joe was yelling at me again, this time for inviting Kenneth. I chose not to remind Joe that I had invited Kenneth, but not him; that he had in fact aggressively invited himself. When you know you're about to collect a million dollars from a losing player, you check your ego at the door.

I didn't want to ask Derek if he was still coming on the Vegas trip, because it would have been unwise and insensitive. In fact I knew I couldn't ask him at all: he would have to let me know. When it comes to games or love, men hate being chased. The problem was that the whole trip was based around Derek and the casino's lust for him. To Blake and his house, Derek was the ultimate whale, and I needed to deliver him. The plane, the villa . . . all the amenities I had secured were contingent on Derek showing up.

IF VEGAS WAS GOING TO HAPPEN, I only had a few days to get a million things done. I wasn't sleeping, and I was running on adrenaline and fumes. I just needed everything to be easy for a second because suddenly nothing was.

I walked into the bank and sat down at my personal banker's desk, placing a stack of cash there for deposit as usual. I smiled at her. She did not smile back.

"Did you get our correspondence?" She sounded uncomfortable.

"No, I haven't had time to go through my mail. Why?"

"I'm very sorry, Molly, but we can't allow you to bank here anymore." Her British accent was crisp.

"Why? What do you mean?" I stammered.

"It's your business." Even with the English lilt firmly in place, her tone was flat.

"I'm an event planner, I pay my taxes, I'm incorporated. What could possibly be the problem?" My heart was in my stomach.

She paused, and then in a low whisper she said, "They know about the poker."

At that moment the bank manager walked over, and my anxiety level shot even higher.

"Miss Bloom, may I have a word?"

"I'm kind of in a hurry," I said, wanting to get out of there as fast as possible. I was half expecting a SWAT team to storm the bank.

"I'll be quick," he said, firmly communicating that it was more of a required chat than an optional one.

I followed him into his office.

"I *am* sorry, Miss Bloom, but we *need* to close out the accounts and you *need* to empty out your safety deposit box." He enunciated his words carefully.

"I don't understand."

"We just *don't* want your kind of *business*."

Jesus, I was running a poker game, not a brothel.

"I'm going to close your account and cut you a check. Please go clear the contents of your safety deposit box. *Now*."

In just minutes, I had gone from shocked to scared to humiliated.

I dutifully walked downstairs and emptied the cash in my box into my handbag. I tried to shove the rubber-banded stacks far into my purse to conceal them, but there was a lot of money and I couldn't close the bag all the way, so I draped my jacket over my purse and returned upstairs, where it felt like the whole bank was staring at me.

The bank manager handed me a check and walked me to the door.

"We *won't* be seeing you here again, Miss Bloom, is that *understood*?"

I nodded and walked quickly to my car.

THE INCIDENT AT THE BANK FRIGHTENED ME, but when I spoke to my attorney, he wasn't the least bit concerned. Nevertheless, the fact that my job was far enough in the gray that I could be blacklisted at a bank was not lost on me.

Meanwhile, I was on pins and needles about whether or not Derek Frost was going to show for my Vegas trip. I left him alone, but I dispatched the girls to express to him how much they wanted to "hang with him" this weekend. I had to behave like it didn't matter if Derek came or not. If he felt he was being pursued, he would make things much more difficult for me. Because let's face it, if Vegas wants you that badly, they're betting on you losing a lot of money.

My gut told me Derek would show, and if he didn't, I had nine other very big gamblers in tow and Blake, the casino host, would just have to deal with it. I knew that Blake had only shared Derek's contact info so that I could do the legwork for him and get him to play at the casino. I was beginning to understand angles.

Blake called while I was packing to say that the plane was waiting for us at the private hangar at LAX.

My doorman called up to inform me that the car was downstairs.

I bit my lip. Still no Derek.

I jumped in the car, where the girls were waiting in all of their tousled goddess glory.

"Vegasssss!" they squealed, and hugged me hello.

"Has anyone spoken to Derek?" I asked.

They hadn't. We drove onto the tarmac and boarded the plane, where a relaxed-looking Derek was sitting, waiting for us.

I gave him an enthusiastic hug, and held on a little too long.

"I better win this weekend," he said as I buckled in. "Or I seriously quit."

I nodded earnestly. No matter how many times these guys swore they were done, they always came back.

VEGAS WAS PERFECT. The villa was magnificent, like the temple of a Roman god. The girls had a great time. The players had an even better time. The game went off well, the guys put in plenty of play at the tables, and no one, including Derek Frost, lost too much.

I had to literally peel them off the tables in order to make it to the plane back to Los Angeles.

Still, no matter how smoothly things went, I was fretting down to the very last minute. Not even when we were back on the plane, on the runway, could I relax. Vegas had been a huge success, but now I had the tournament to worry about. As I looked around at the happy, sleepy people surrounding me on the leather seats, I thought about all of the behind-the-scenes work I'd had to do to make their fun look effortless. While everyone around me dozed, I gazed out the window and calculated all the things that I would have to do in the coming days.

There was a game on Tuesday, a tournament on Wednesday, and another game on Thursday. I had a lot of logistics to manage, and not enough time to do all the things I needed to do. It didn't matter. The rest of my life was going to have to wait. Including my boyfriend, who was getting tired of feeling like he was less important than the game. My family and old friends, who didn't understand why I never called them back anymore. Reardon and the guys, who had watched me become this new person. And my dog, who would be faithful no matter what.

Chapter 22

I had never staged a tournament before, but Diego had, and he was a hugely valuable resource. There were just so many things to think about, and it all had to go right in order for the day to be a success. All of the guys seemed excited; Houston Curtis showed up to play, even though his wife's birthday party was being held that evening and I knew that he had been planning the bash for quite some time.

The players counted their wins in hands and chips. I counted mine in players. The turnout was amazing; even Arthur Grossman showed up. He eyed the girls unabashedly, and pulled me aside to whisper-ask who they were.

"Oh, friends of mine," I explained, and he watched them for a few more minutes before he went over to chat with Tobey.

Arthur busted out of the tournament quickly, and as soon as he sat down at the cash game, I saw some of the guys who were still in the tournament scrambling to lose all their chips so that they could join him at the cash game. They understood that the real upside would come from playing Arthur in a no-limit game, not a tournament with a set amount of chips. Arthur called me over in between hands.

"I'm going to start playing on a weekly basis," he said. "Please let me know when the games will be."

"You got it," I said, as if nothing major had just happened. Arthur had dropped in and out. Now I would have him at the table week after week. He was the dream recruit: a guy who had an endless bankroll, an endless ego, and, as far as I could tell, extremely limited skills

A FEW HOURS INTO THE TOURNAMENT, the only person who wasn't having fun was Tobey. I had let him craft the structure of the tournament to accommodate his playing style, and he had pushed as hard as he could for it, but sometimes you just can't win, no matter how good you are. Sometimes you just get unlucky. Tobey had hit a losing streak, which for him meant he had lost at two hands. He looked sullen, a sure sign that he was about to start complaining.

He had taken to criticizing me about everything under the sun, especially how much I was making in my role. As my influence had increased, and my tips, so had his harping.

I didn't like this. Tobey was powerful and tactical. There was a tiny nagging voice in the back of my head that was telling me that Tobey being unhappy spelled trouble for me, but I tried to stay focused. The games were good. No, they were great. They were becoming legendary, and I told myself as long as I kept them at this level, my role was safe, no matter how much he whined. To make matters worse, Houston Curtis was losing as well. The party he had planned for his wife's birthday started at nine.

Nine P.M. came and went, and then ten.

"Houston," I whispered in his ear. "You have to go. You have the party."

"Not now, Molly," he said, eyes on the cards.

By early morning, ten hours into playing, Tobey and Houston were both stuck for half a million. I hoped Houston would cut his losses and go home; he had already missed his wife's birthday and he had certainly won enough over the last couple years to be able to absorb a $500,000 loss. But the two who never lost were battling it out, and neither showed any sign of quitting anytime soon.

Rick Salomon and Andrew Sasson were there too, both immensely enjoying the unlikely scenario of Tobey and Houston down $1 million at 5 A.M. Andrew was a feisty Brit who had started out working doors at clubs, and had used his knowledge, relationships, and mouth to create his own club in Vegas and was now in negotiations to sell his company for $80 million.

I liked him, even though he was cantankerous and miserable. He respected my hustle, and always, or almost always, treated me with respect and kindness. He also wasn't afraid to offend or insult anyone, even the celebrities, which was a refreshing attribute in this town.

I also liked Rick. He was crass and he embraced his nickname, "Scum," but he was honest and fair.

Rick and Andrew were living it up, talking shit to Houston and Tobey. Tobey was smiling, but I could see in his eyes that he was not happy.

"All in," Tobey said suddenly.

"Call," said Houston.

I looked at Houston. His eyes were wild. The normal discipline was gone. He was out of control. I knew that he could not truly afford to gamble with these guys . . . usually Houston played good poker, which meant skill, psychology, and statistics, all very different from footloose gambling.

Diego turned over the cards.

Tobey had him crushed from the beginning. Houston had gone all in with nothing.

My radar kicked into gear. Houston was one of the only players who didn't have an endless bankroll. I hadn't worried because in the beginning he'd been staked by Tobey, and he won on such a consistent basis. But after winning a couple million, he had bought himself out from Tobey. He had made enough money to play on his own and he wanted to realize all his wins and not just a portion.

Tobey had made a ton of money off Houston in the last couple years. It was pretty safe to assume that Tobey wasn't thrilled about it when Houston bought him out.

Now Tobey had just gotten even, and Houston was down a million.

Andrew and Rick were laughing like hyenas. There was a ton of animosity toward Houston in the game, because the guys resented that he was making a fortune off them.

Tobey stood up, smiling from ear to ear.

"Well, thanks, good buddy," he said, smacking a devastated Houston on the back.

"You're leaving, bro?" Houston asked incredulously. "I just got you even and you're leaving?"

"Yep," said Tobey, without a trace of apology in his voice. "Thanks, though."

He smiled and plopped his chips in front of me.

"Phew," he said, with a look that meant I should be as relieved as he was.

I smiled back.

"Nice," I said, even though in the end Houston had virtually handed Tobey the win.

I hated myself for being so disloyal. I had been rooting hard for Houston. But I knew my job security depended largely on Tobey's wins.

"Thanks," he said, smiling like we were partners.

"Seriously? You're leaving?" Houston asked, sounding plaintive.

"I'm tired," Tobey said, looking delighted.

His eyes were wide open and alert and I didn't believe him for a second, but it was his right to go. He had met his usual four-and-a-half-hour play limit, and exceeded it by five and a half hours. I knew he wanted to book the win, and while, in my opinion, it may have not been ethical to get up directly after that hand, it was certainly allowed.

Tobey seemed gleeful as he practically skipped out the door.

HOUSTON WAS OUT OF CHIPS, and Rick and Andrew were having the time of their lives.

Houston approached.

"Give me five hundred K," he said.

"Come talk to me." I motioned him over to a quiet corner.

Making my decision wasn't easy. Houston was down a million in this particular game, but he had won millions from these guys over the last couple years. Rick and Andrew would resent me if I didn't extend credit, since Houston's millions had come from their pockets. The Houston I had come to know as a player could certainly take these guys and get back to even, but this game's Houston I didn't believe in.

"Houston, call it. You aren't playing well. You're tilted the fuck out. I've never seen you play so badly. You played a dead hand for half a million!"

"I know, it was stupid," he said. "I had a read. I'm not usually wrong. I'm good for it, Mol! I've always tipped you twenty percent. You know I'm good for it."

Every cell in my body told me not to do it, but I didn't know how I could say no. According to the playbooks, he had won more than enough to justify any debt to me.

"Five hundred K and that's it," I said. At the end of the day, I had caught a lot of flak for allowing Houston to play and consistently win. I knew I wouldn't lose him as a player if he lost; I also knew it wasn't fair to the other guys not to give them the chance to win back some of their money from him.

"Okay," he said. "I can do it. I swear, these guys are donkeys."

"Just don't be stupid."

I WALKED OUT WITH HOUSTON and counted out $500,000 in chips. I had twenty messages from a "too tired" Tobey, and a couple from Bob Safai, who'd left around 2 A.M. but now wanted to buy back in. I knew these guys smelled blood and wanted to be a part of the feeding frenzy.

Rick and Andrew cheered when Houston sat back down.

Diego and I exchanged glances. None of this was good.

It didn't take long for Houston to lose his stack. His play hadn't changed and I realized that if he had been sitting there with $10 million, he would have lost it all.

He walked over to me, dejected, downtrodden, and asking me for more chips.

"Not today, Houston, go home. Go be with your wife."

He had missed her birthday completely. I watched him walk out and I wanted to cry for him. I had a heavy feeling of guilt. I thought I could mine the good parts of gambling and elude the dark, but I was wrong.

OVER THE COMING WEEKS, Houston confessed to me that he had borrowed the money to cover his losses from Tobey, at terrible terms. According to Houston, the deal was this: Tobey would take all of Houston's wins, none of his losses, to the tune of 50 percent for a year. No poker player can beat that juice, but Houston said he agreed. He could have procured much better options. There were plenty of people who would have staked him for better terms . . . hell, he could have gotten money on the street for better terms. But I think he realized, like I had, that staying in Tobey's good graces was essential to staying in the game. If what Houston told me was true, Tobey owned Houston now, and they must have both known it. Houston constantly looked stressed. He owned 100 percent of his downside and was only realizing 50 percent of his wins, and he was the only one at the table who was playing for his mortgage.

"I'm going to make ten million this year on poker!" Tobey once exclaimed, not knowing that I knew that Houston had told me about the alleged arrangement they had.

For a short time Tobey seemed to forgot about his disenchantment with my escalating income. He was back to pushing for even more games, and back to acting like my best buddy.

For the moment my position was safe, but Houston was on a downward spiral and I was certain it wouldn't end well.

Chapter 23

We were at another insane game, and I was watching Guy Laliberté convince another player to fold a winning hand. Guy was a huge gambler, aggressive and ruthless at a table. He had started his life as a scrappy street performer, literally doing tricks for his dinner, until he had the idea to start a circus-themed live performance and now his little company, Cirque du Soleil, made him a billion dollars a year. This other player was a nice East Coast guy who had made a bunch of money trading stocks. He was a real gentleman and seemed out of his element with the antics of the L.A. game.

Tobey was losing again, so, of course, he was back to disapproving of me, my tips, and the game in general. Now he was in for $250,000, down to his last $50,000, and trying to dig his way out. Jamie Gold was once again playing like it was his last day on earth, and Tobey knew his best shot of getting out of the hole was Jamie.

Jamie and Tobey were all in and I wasn't sure which one I was rooting for. Jamie had almost lost his bankroll from his World Series win, and once he did, I wouldn't be able to let him play anymore. I liked Jamie, he was kind and generous. Tobey was the worst tipper, the biggest winner, and the absolute worst loser, but I had to worry about my job security if he lost. I held my breath and watched Diego turn over the cards. Tobey won.

Predictably, Tobey stood up immediately after the hand that made him whole. "Well, that's it for me." He came over to me and set his stacks on my clipboard.

"Whew, you're lucky I won that hand," he said, crinkling his eyes and using his usual half-kidding/half-serious/you-guess-which tone.

I nodded.

"You have to cut Jamie off, you know."

"I know," I said, counting his chips.

He held a thousand-dollar chip in his hand. He flipped it over a couple times in his fingers.

"This is yours," he said, holding it out to me.

"Thanks, Tobey," I said, reaching my hand out.

He yanked the chip back at the last second.

"If . . ." he said. "If you do something to earn these thousand dollars." His voice was loud enough that some of the guys looked up to see what was happening.

I laughed, trying not to show my nerves.

"What do I want you to do?" he said, as if he were pondering.

The whole table was watching us now.

"I know!" he said. "Get up on that desk and bark like a seal."

I looked at him. His face was lit up like it was Christmas Eve.

"Bark like a seal who wants a fish," he said.

I laughed again, stalling, hoping he would play the joke out by himself and leave.

"I'm not kidding. What's wrong? You're too rich now? You won't bark for a thousand dollars? Wowwww . . . you must be really rich."

My face was burning. The room was silent.

"C'mon," he said, holding the chip above my head. "BARK."

"No," I said quietly

"NO?" he asked.

"Tobey," I said. "I'm not going to bark like a seal. Keep your chip."

My face was on fire. I knew he would be angry, especially because he had now engaged the whole audience, and I wasn't playing his game. I was embarrassed, but I was also angry. After all I had done to accommodate this guy, I was also shocked. I made sure I ran every detail of every game by him, changed the stakes for him, structured tournaments around him, had memorized every ingredient in every vegan dish in town for him. He had won millions and millions of dollars at my table and I had catered to his every need along the way—and now he seemed to want to humiliate me.

He kept pushing it, his voice growing louder and louder. The other guys were starting to look uncomfortable.

"No," I said, again, willing him to drop it.

He gave me an icy look, dropped the chip on the table, and tried to laugh it off, but he was visibly angry.

When he left, the room was buzzing.

"What was that?"

"So weird."

"Glad you didn't do it, Molly."

I knew it was more than a childish tantrum. It had been a challenge because Tobey wanted to show that he was the alpha. I knew I hadn't made the most strategic decision by refusing to submit, but I also needed to retain the respect of the other players.

FOR THE FIRST TIME SINCE THE GAME BEGAN, I realized that it could end. So, in all likelihood, did Tobey. He had anticipated everything except the dip in the economy and how much money Diego and I were making, and our take-home seemed to be eating him up.

He began bringing up how much I was making even more frequently, not even trying to hide his dissatisfaction.

"I think the game needs restructuring," he said one night.

"How so?"

"Well, you make too much and it takes too long to get paid."

I raised my eyebrows. In what other universe do you show up, play a game, win a MILLION DOLLARS, and get the check within a week? The only reason this game was still running was that I had searched far and wide to recruit new blood and maintain relationships so that Tobey could take their money. Now he had the balls to suggest that I figure out a way to cap my own salary.

I smiled at him.

"I'll look into it," I murmured.

"Thanks," he said.

IT WAS THE END OF THE SUMMER and Hillary and Obama were battling for the Democratic nomination. I wanted Hillary to win, but I didn't believe she would. Meanwhile, Tobey was a staunch and passionate supporter of Obama, and he had bet substantial money on his candidate. These guys loved side action. I even saw them make a substantial bet on Kobayashi, the Japanese hot-dog-eating champion. It gave me an idea.

"I'll take Hillary," I said one evening, during a game.

I was sadly pretty sure that Hillary would lose, but I thought that if I let Tobey best me, I could regain my edge. I knew that he was powerful. He was an A-lister in Hollywood who knew how to leverage his celebrity, and since he seemed to only do movies for people who would agree to his over-the-top demands, he had a lot of time on his hands. And he had an incredibly obsessive mind. He was the last person in the world who I wanted to set up to take me down.

But if I let Tobey beat me, I hoped, maybe he would feel better about my tips. Especially if it was a very public "defeat."

Tobey's head snapped up and his eyes brightened.

"Realllly? How much?"

"I think Hillary is definitely going to win," I lied.

"So you're confident?"

"Very." I had learned to bluff from the best (and worst) of them.

"So let's bet ten thousand."

"Okay," I said evenly.

Diego looked at me like I was insane.

"What are you doing?" he mouthed.

Saving our jobs, I thought, grinning like I had the upper hand while I shrugged off the discomfort of putting $10,000 on a losing bet.

"Are you really going to take her money?" Bob asked, squinting at Tobey in distaste.

"YOU BET!" Tobey exclaimed.

DREW AND I HAD PLANNED A TRIP to Aspen for New Year's. I was distracted the whole time, thinking about the shadow of current events that was looming over my good fortune. The only thing people seemed to discuss anymore was the ailing economy. I tried to ignore it but it was everywhere, and the general consensus was that things were going to get a lot worse.

Between Tobey's disenchantment and the ominous threat of an economic crash, I couldn't shake the uneasiness. I poured myself a glass of scotch and tried to relax.

"Tell us about the game, Molly. Who wins the most?"

I looked away from the horizon and toward the questioner, a guy named Paul, and smiled at him. It was no longer a secret that I ran the biggest poker game in the city, and though I maintained discretion about the important aspects, I had recently begun playing to the crowd whenever the role presented itself.

I dressed like a woman and looked like a woman, but I could speak the language of men fluently. They were intrigued by my game, by my lifestyle, and by the crew of girls that I employed. I now drove a Bentley, I split the cost of the private jets, I threw in for tables at the club. I had hired a personal assistant to do all my chores, I had a chef, and all the minutiae and mundane tasks had been removed from my daily life. So had my closest relationships. I hadn't spoken to Blair or anyone from my past in ages. I never called them, and they had stopped calling me, one by one. My family knew I was running poker games, and they were aware I was making (and spending) a lot of money, but I tried to avoid the topic with them whenever possible. They disapproved of my career path. I decided I didn't need them to approve.

Some girls have hearts and stars in their eyes. I had dollar signs. I handled the money, the recruitment of new players. I was perpetually on the lookout for new deals, new opportunities. I was the lifeblood of the game and it was mine. And because of my increased role, I had recently reduced Diego's take from 50 to 25 percent. After all, I was the one risking everything, acting as the bank, and I was the one who found the players and kept them happy. Diego was just a dealer who showed up, did his job, and left. For me it was 24/7. Still, I felt a nagging sense of guilt.

Diego was understandably upset.

"The only thing that will fuck this up is greed," he said, though he accepted his fate. His words echoed in my head now, and I felt the guilt rising.

Grow up, Molly, I told myself. This isn't high school, it's not a popularity contest. This is part of being a businesswoman. It's just business, I thought. This phrase was a useful way to justify behaving with greed instead of compassion. I had been using it a lot lately.

But in my heart of hearts, I felt like I was losing myself.

I downed another glass of scotch. I didn't want to look inside, didn't want to think about who I was or who I had become. I wanted to enjoy the life that I had worked so hard to build.

We all drank, and I regaled my captive audience with tales from the table. I saw Drew out of the corner of my eye frowning at my display, but I pretended not to notice.

IT WAS NOW IMPOSSIBLE to keep my personal life and my poker life separate. I slept with both of my BlackBerries on my chest; one for poker and one for everything else. Many times, I would crawl out of Drew's bed in the middle of the night to deal with an issue or collect. The players took precedence. My relationship suffered for it . . . but the rule was, if a gambler calls you at 4 A.M. and says they have cash or a check, you get up and go, because by four fifteen it could be gone. That was just how it was.

Gone were the nights Drew and I would share a bottle of wine, shut the little Italian restaurant down, and never run out of things to talk or laugh about. He too was facing issues that were stressing him; although he never spoke about it, I could feel a change. He seemed unhappy, unsatisfied. I felt a distance settle firmly between us.

When we finally ended our workweeks, instead of enjoying each other or luxuriating in much-needed sleep, Drew and I joined our friends for dinner at trendy restaurants and then went to the clubs, where we both got lost in the loud music and the endless flow of alcohol. My life had become all about the hustle and the party. Drew started going out more without me, especially on the nights I was working. Then he started taking "boys' trips" without me. I knew what happened on those trips. I spent my life in poker rooms and I had gotten an education no woman wants. I trusted him, but I missed the days when he wanted me to come along.

IT WAS THE FIRST WEEK OF JUNE and Drew and I had planned to spend the summer at his beach house in Malibu again. I was hoping we could get back to the old us.

He had gone out in the city the night before. We were supposed to have dinner with his parents tonight. He was late and I was getting antsy. I went for a long walk on the beach, the sun was setting, and it was incredibly beautiful. Drew still wasn't there when I got back.

I was starting to get worried, his phone was going straight to voice mail every time I called.

Just then I got a call from a strange number.

"Mollll," Drew slurred.

"Where are you?"

His answer was jumbled. I heard laughing in the background.

"I'm gonna stay in the city," he yelled above the noise. "Come."

We both knew he didn't mean it.

"It's beautiful out here," I tried, even though I knew it was a lost cause. "And we have dinner with your family planned. Want me to pick you up?"

I heard a shuffle and then the line went dead.

Tears of frustration filled my eyes. But the frustration quickly turned to pain, because as much as I didn't want to face what I had known for a while, my relationship was over. I couldn't pretend anymore. A reel of the past two and a half years ran behind my eyes. Drew was my first love. I thought about the beginning, when our relationship was sweet and inno-cent. When I thought that he could be the one.

I walked out onto the beach and sat at the water's edge. I knew what I had to do. I knew it because it was right for both of us. He needed to be young and single, and I wasn't really in a position to be anyone's girlfriend because of my job. I hugged my knees to my chest and felt a pang of fear at the thought of losing him forever. I couldn't imagine my life without him. Drew was more than my boyfriend—he had become my best friend and my family.

DREW FINALLY ARRIVED AT THE HOUSE late the next afternoon while I was lying on the beach. I didn't even ask where he had been. I choked back my tears.

He walked outside and started to apologize.

I grabbed his hand.

"It's okay, it's just time. You need to be young and I need to focus on my work." He turned his head and for a moment I thought I saw his eyes get wet. He wrapped his arms around me and I cried onto his chest. He held me, but I knew he agreed. We sat like that for a long time.

I put my hands over my eyes and sobbed. I didn't know how to leave; I felt like the second I walked out the door, nothing would ever be the same. I would never kiss him again, or wake up with him next to me. After everything we shared, our life together would just end.

I walked into the house and started packing in the bedroom, shaking with sobs, silently begging him to stop me, to plead with me to stay. But he just waited in the living room.

I stood in front of him with my bags packed and I could tell by his eyes and his posture he was already gone. He didn't even get up to hug me good-bye.

"I love you, I'll always love you," I choked, and I walked out of his life.

At home in my empty, quiet house, I got into bed and hugged Lucy. It was Saturday night and all my friends were out. It had been such a long time since I was home alone on a weekend.

In order to run the game I had learned how to be strong, brave, and to suppress my emotional side. I had learned to read the players and play my own tactical game.

But that night I was stripped of my armor; I was just a girl alone in a big city with a broken heart.

Walking away from Drew was the most mature, most difficult decision of my adult life. There was no trauma, no drama, no closure. It was just time. We had gotten as close as our lives and our dysfunction would permit.

Chapter 24

I buried myself in work. The game became the only thing that mattered, but I could feel the shadows creeping in. Diego was no longer my ally. Tobey seemed obsessed with the money I was making. The economy was officially spiraling out of control and I knew my players who made their money on Wall Street and real estate were being affected.

This culminated in a call from Arthur's office. It was his assistant.

"Hi, Molly, it's Virginia. Arthur wants to know if you mind if he has the game at his house this Tuesday."

It wasn't really a question.

"Sure, no problem, what time should I come over to set up?"

"Oh no, don't worry. Arthur says you don't have to work. He'll just pay you."

There was an uncomfortable silence.

"It'll be like a paid vacation," she said, with an awkward laugh.

"Okay," I said brightly, covering up what I really felt, which was ice-cold fear.

This was bad, really bad. Maybe Arthur was being honest, and he just wanted to host for one night at his house. He had just finished construction on an $85 million mansion and maybe he just wanted to show it off. I had hosted plenty of games at other people's houses. The big red flag was that he didn't want me there. He was planning to use my staff, my buy-in sheets, my table, my Shuffle Master, and my dealer.

It was my game without me.

ON TUESDAY NIGHT, I tried to go out with my girlfriends, but every second ripped me apart. My game was happening, and I wasn't there. It was a pointless exercise to try to have fun, and I was in no mood to be out, so I went home and waited.

Finally, at 2 A.M., my phone rang. It was Tobey.

"You're fucked," he said gleefully.

"What does that mean, exactly?" I asked, trying not to cry.

"Arthur wants to have the game at his house from now on." He sounded a little gentler when he heard the emotion in my voice.

It was obvious that this excluded me.

"Every week?" I asked, assessing the damage.

"Yeah."

I was silent for a moment, trying to swallow the lump in my throat and keep from crying.

"Thanks for the heads-up." I attempted to sound casual, but the words caught in my throat and the tears were coming hard and fast.

"I'll try to talk to him for you," he said awkwardly.

"Thank you," I sniffled, wanting to believe him.

"I'm sorry," he said, as if he had just realized that I was a real person with real feelings.

I hung up and forced myself to focus on finding a solution. I would just call Arthur and schedule a meeting. I would explain the whole situation. He seemed like a reasonable guy. There had to be some way to come to a compromise. I tried to fall asleep but my mind was racing.

I would just deal with this head-on, I thought, and speak to him like a human being. Explain what the game meant to me, how much I had risked and sacrificed, and explain to him the amount of work I regularly did in the background. He was a self-made businessman, an entrepreneur, surely he would understand.

His secretary answered my call. She took my name, and when she came back on the line, her voice was cold.

I waited all day and Arthur didn't call back. I e-mailed him, no response. I e-mailed his assistant, no response.

Meanwhile, many of the guys called to apologize and explain.

"Mol, if Arthur wasn't such a huge fish . . ."

"I mean he's going to *donate* twenty million this year."

"He's such a donkey."

No matter how good I was at my job, this game was about money and I couldn't compete with a guy who lost millions at the table.

ARTHUR HOSTED THE GAME THAT WEEK, and the next, and pretty soon a month of Tuesdays had gone by in similar fashion. Each week I sent out my invitation text, and each week I received apologetic no's. I battled the urge to stay in bed all day and cry. I needed a plan. I couldn't passively wait for the tide to turn—I needed to turn it myself. I had a few options.

I could show up at Arthur's and beg him to give me a job at the new game. I heard he had his accountant running the books and employed the latest model/actress he was pursuing to serve drinks. The whole thing made me sick. I knew the game would never be mine again.

I could try to build a new game in L.A.

Or I could go somewhere else.

L.A. was full of ghosts. Drew, the game, and the friends I had traded for my new life. But leaving was about more than walking away from a poker game: this event had been my identity, my proof that I was really, really good at something. I had built my identity and my future upon Reardon, Drew, and the Los Angeles Dodgers; now even the foundation was falling into itself. Sometimes a stupid fairy tale about pigs and building houses is more timeless than a living, breathing, tangible world that seemed forever and indestructible.

ONE OF THE WORST MISTAKES a poker player can make is not knowing when to fold. I had spent thousands of hours watching guys stay in hands too long, stay too late on nights when they were running so cold they couldn't win a hand. I knew that most poker truths were applicable to real life, and although the thought of it crushed me, I knew it was time to walk away.

I grieved for a night or two and then I got angry—and anger felt better than sadness, more powerful. I could see Los Angeles clearly now . . . it was the kind of town where people came to prove themselves and their worth, dedicated to the pursuit of their own amazingness. Either you climbed to the top and then fought with all of your energy to hang on, looking at everyone around you with suspicion while accepting their fawning admiration, or you let the victors chew you up and spit you out, nourishing themselves on your weakness. This town was not made for permanence. It was designed for the quick flare of genius, the sputter and die when a new genius came along. That's not how it was going to be with me.

Ever since my trip east with the McCourts, I had dreamed of New York City. It was time to go.

Part Five
A CHIP
AND A CHAIR

New York, 2009–May 2010

A Chip and a Chair (noun)

An expression that means that as long as you have a single chip and a seat at the table in a poker tournament, you can still come back.

Chapter 25

*A*nd so New York City it was. I thought about the magnitude of the place. About the mythical game that was five times the size of mine. The only shot I had at infiltrating was Kenneth Redding, the Wall Street tycoon who had bullied the hell out of even Tobey at the poker table. I had made sure to promptly collect his million and a half and have it wired to him before he turned his G-5 around and landed in the city. And later, when he crushed my game for another million, I paid him quickly—even though I had to cover some of it personally.

I picked up my phone and called him, and he answered on the first ring.

"Molllyyyyyy," he cooed. "How are you? Are you running around in a bikini with your girlfriends?"

Yuck.

"Of course we are. In fact we're at the pool right now talking about you."

"About me? Oh, I love that. So, what can I do for you?"

"L.A. is getting boring, Kenneth," I said. "We need a change of scenery."

I FLEW TO NEW YORK to test out the waters with Tiffany, the model/playmate I had met on the trip to Vegas I took with Drew. She had become one of my closest friends, and she was street-smart in a way you couldn't teach—but she was so beautiful that no one saw it coming behind those big blue eyes.

According to Kenneth, the big game in New York didn't happen very often because it was such a pain to organize. When I suggested taking over the "burden" of organizing, he said that personally, he would love this, but the other guys might not be on board. I asked if I could come to the game and meet them to try to win them over. Kenneth agreed.

I decided to stay at the Four Seasons again. Of course, when I walked into the hotel, memories of Drew flooded my head. I remembered staring at the Manhattan skyline, being in love for the first time. So, in order to divert my attention, Tiffany and I went out to explore the city, hitting up the hottest clubs, restaurants, and bars. To strangers we looked like a couple of party girls, but actually we were on the hunt for contacts, information, and networks we could tap into.

Everyone we talked to loved the idea of a poker game "run by hot girls," and in two short days we had enough names to get started.

The big game was scheduled for my final night in town, and I went alone. This time, I dressed the part of a CEO instead of a party girl. I wore a blazer over my black dress, and my glasses, which I hoped made me look older and more intellectual. I wanted to be taken seriously.

I sat in the backseat for a moment after my cab pulled up outside the town house on Park Avenue, the home of one of the biggest guys on Wall Street and the location of the game. I knew this would be a daunting room. This game was full of larger-than-life, masters-of-the-finance-universe types who had been playing together for legendary amounts for a decade and a half. The guys in L.A. may have starred in or directed movies, but these were the guys who wrote the checks to fund those movies, and when they made moves the whole financial market followed.

A MAN IN A TAILORED SUIT escorted me through a gorgeous foyer and down a small back stairway that led to a small, unfinished basement. This was not at all what I had expected. These were some of the world's richest men, and they were playing the biggest game I had ever heard of. These were distinguished gentlemen dressed in custom suits, and they were playing on a makeshift table with cheap chips and mismatched chairs.

Kenneth introduced me to the players. I had already been briefed. They gave me a smattering of polite but aloof greetings, and I settled back in my seat to watch.

I already knew plenty about Kenneth himself. He was one of the most powerful men on Wall Street, and his connections and success were unprecedented. He had called me one evening to ask if I could get a reservation for three: for himself, Steve Jobs, and Bill Gates. He still wanted to impress the guys at the games and make sure that they ran perfectly. He knew I would make sure that happened.

Easton Brandt, the host, was a self-made billionaire who owned a gigantic hedge fund that contained billions in assets. Next to Easton was Keith Finkle, a legend back in the days when trading on the floor could make or break careers. He had made an obscene amount of money and parlayed it into his own fund and numerous real-estate investments. Helly Nahmad sat to Keith's left. A well-known playboy who dated actual supermodels, he ran around with Leonardo DiCaprio and his crew. Helly's family owned the world's largest collection of classical art, valued conservatively at $3 billion.

In seat five was Illya. Rumor had it that Illya's father, Vadim, ran the largest bookmaking operation in the world, taking bets from his closest oligarch friends in Russia. Illya was the prodigy son who had shown up in New York a couple years prior with a backpack of a million in cash and a cover story about his family's steel business. He lost every dollar in poker, went back to the smaller stakes, built up his bankroll, and after a couple months completely dominated the game. Next to him was Igor, a short, fiery Russian who was allegedly staked by Vadim. And finally, there were the twins. Each of these identical brothers spent most of the game harassing the other, and it wasn't a friendly banter. When either twin lost a big pot or suffered a bad hand, the other was genuinely delighted.

I stayed quietly in my corner observing. Kenneth was in a $4 million hand with Illya. I silently added the stacks in my head.

Jesus.

I looked around to see if they had anyone working the game. There was an older English gentleman who appeared to be a butler, an older white-haired gentleman dealing the cards, and a dark-eyed kid in his early twenties, dressed in sagging pants with a hat pushed down over his eyes. He watched the game intently, and appeared to be in charge of the rebuys.

I held my breath as the dealer dealt the "river," or final card. Kenneth lost. I waited for him to explode, order the dealer to be fired, or ban me for life; the type of theatrics that often took place at my L.A. game. Instead he casually pushed his chips to Illya, barely pausing in his conversation with Easton Brandt.

I stared in disbelief. This was a gentleman's game, and at least on the surface, the civilized men at the table seemed completely unconcerned by the crashing economy that had the rest of the world on tilt.

After I had spent enough time observing, I left to meet Tiffany, who was having drinks with some of the potential players we had met over the week.

My mind was racing. I had just been given entry into the biggest home game in the world. For fifteen years the finance world had been whispering about this secret, magical game, and I knew the secret: it might have had the reputation of an Ivy League secret club, a Skull and Bones society, but it felt more like game night at the frat house, albeit with millions backing the chips. I knew that I could impress these men with aesthetic details and service, but if there was anything that I had learned from my life in L.A., it was that winning counted more than ambience. I needed to add serious value: new, easy-money players, interesting or hard-to-access people, like celebrities, professional athletes. Add impeccable math, and timely collections and payouts, plus beautiful girls and a beautiful setting. It could work.

Chapter 26

Kenneth called me the next day to say that the guys had agreed to give me a trial run.

That was all I needed.

"Make sure you bring the girls—oh, and get rid of Eugene. He's Illya's brother, but there's no need for him," Kenneth said in clipped tones.

"Okay."

I felt a twinge of guilt about Eugene, the kid with the cap covering his face who was watching the rebuys. He seemed like a good guy, lost in his big brother's shadow and just trying to be part of his world.

But if that was what Kenneth and his friends wanted, that was what they would get.

Plus, I had more important things to think about. I would be hosting my debut game in New York. I had one shot to prove myself. I flew back to L.A. to get ready.

First, I had the L.A. Four Seasons make a call to its sister hotel in New York City and arrange the most beautiful room they had for me. Then I got in touch with each of the players' assistants to learn which drinks, food, and cigars I needed to have on hand. Next, I needed to find the girls whom I could hire to staff the game, and most importantly I needed to find at least two new players who were either celebrities and or would bring a ton of action.

Miraculously, I put all the pieces together. I invited Guy Laliberté, and he readily agreed to come. He had a passion for poker so great that even when he was losing he was cheerful. I also invited A-Rod. There was nothing like a legendary professional athlete to turn a bunch of tough, successful guys into starry-eyed little girls.

WHEN WE LANDED AT JFK, the girls and I went straight to the hotel.

We gasped aloud at the room, which was unbelievable. The floor-to-ceiling windows provided a 360-degree view of Manhattan. Each room in the 4,300-square-foot suite was more impressive than the next. A baby grand piano sat elegantly in the middle of the living room and sparkling chandeliers hung from the twenty-foot ceilings.

I had barely put my bags down when my phone rang. It was a local pro I knew from L.A. He had made it a point to introduce himself several times. He badly wanted into my L.A. game. I was always polite but I would never have let him in.

"Hi," I said.

"You won't be able to do games in New York City," he told me, guessing my intentions accurately. "You should go home. New York is different."

Was that a threat? It certainly wasn't friendly advice. I chose to ignore the implicit warning, because, as far as I was concerned, this guy was nothing more than a harmless opportunist.

"Eddie runs shit here," he continued.

I also knew who Eddie Ting was. Eddie had grown up in the underground poker scene. He had started out as a player at one-dollar, two-dollar tables, and he was good enough that he had soon saved enough of a bankroll to start his own games. My take on it was that he was a shrewd businessman who seemed to care only about profit, and he would step on anyone to get ahead. Eddie had run a couple of underground multitable poker clubs back when they were both plentiful and extremely lucrative. Eventually, he became the king of New York poker.

A couple years after I started the L.A. game, Eddie heard about the action and my take, and had tried to get in on it. He rented an apartment and attempted to break into the scene. He wasn't successful and I had heard that he returned to New York with his tail in between his legs. It was very clear that Eddie was less than pleased that I had come here, and according to Illya, he was irate that I had a shot at the big game, one he had been trying to infiltrate for many years.

"Thanks for the advice. Hope you're doing well," I said, and hung up.

I made a mental note to reach out to Eddie and try to clear the air. The last thing I needed was enemies.

THE GIRLS AND I TOOK SPECIAL PAINS getting ready before the game. We knew we were auditioning. Eugene arrived shortly before we started.

"Whoaaa, nice room," he said appreciatively, nodding his head at the view. He was wearing baggy sweatpants, a sweatshirt that said FUCK YOU, PAY ME, and smelled strongly of weed and cigarettes. I wasn't sure if he was simply unaware of the fact that he should at least make an effort to look presentable, or if he just didn't care.

"Hi," I said, and after the pleasantries were over, I told him that I would be doing the chips for this game.

He looked at me with a dark stare.

"Can I still watch?" He spoke plainly, no ass-kissing or awe.

I scrunched my brows. I wanted this night to be perfect and I already knew my MVP, Kenneth, was irritated by his presence.

"I guess," I said. "Just don't stand behind the players. It's distracting."

He shot me a look but he nodded.

By the time the first guy arrived, the girls and I were perfectly poised, with the most decadent hotel room in NYC as our venue. I had purchased a new, top-of-the-line table, with pristine, virgin green felt, mahogany rails with custom cup holders, and, of course, a custom hole for the Shuffle Master. One by one the players came in, men whose reality consisted of expected luxury, except when it was left to them to arrange: like their weekly poker games. The girls turned the charm up to ten. They laughed at jokes, marveled at stories, and accommodated every need, sometimes before the players even thought to ask. I had learned never to underestimate the power of making a man feel special and impressive, so I had done background research and memorized each player's greatest accomplishments, and as the night went on I made sure to ask about them.

They loved the table. The custom chips that were just the right weight and composition. The guys were basking in the attention. The room was on fire. It was so different from the first game I witnessed at Easton Brandt's. It seemed like nothing could go wrong.

Guy arrived, charismatic as usual, and regaling the guys with his incredible story of rags to riches, and they decided to start.

The game kicked off aggressively, with Kenneth going all in first hand and Bernie, a recent addition to the game, Igor, and Illya calling. I sucked in my breath and watched the action.

The first hand of the night was a million dollars.

Meanwhile, someone asked me to turn on the television because Bush was giving his Speech to the Nation on the crumbling economy. It was September 2008, and as I refurbished Igor, Bernie, and Kenneth with another $250,000 each, I couldn't ignore the irony of the speech as a backdrop to the biggest poker game I had ever run.

BERNIE ASKED ME IF HE COULD BUY IN for $50,000. It was my understanding that the minimum buy-in and rebuy was $250,000, so I asked the table if anyone objected. As usual, whenever I asked the table to decide, as opposed to making the call myself, there was a passionate, contentious discussion. A-Rod showed up in the middle of the bickering and the table forgot about the petty squabble and became agreeable almost immediately. I gave Bernie his chips and attended to Alex, who decided to sit and watch for a bit.

"What a game," he said, looking at the chip stacks. Dinner had just arrived and I needed to watch the cardplaying.

I nodded my head. "It's pretty insane."

Luckily, my friend Katherine had just shown up, all six feet, Georgia drawl, tight leather catsuit of her. The men were mesmerized. She took over entertaining A-Rod and I walked back toward the table.

Eugene tapped my shoulder.

"Yo," he said casually. "You didn't write down the fifty for Bernie."

I shot him an annoyed look.

"Yes, I did," I said, indignant.

He was rolling a joint and not even looking at me.

"Nah, you didn't."

I scowled at him. "It's not my first time running a poker game," I said.

He met my glare with confidence, looking at me now with large black almond-shaped eyes.

"Okay, whatever you say."

I grabbed the sheet and dramatically pointed at the box next to Bernie's name.

It was empty.

My eyes opened wide.

Eugene was right. He knew full well that if I succeeded tonight he would lose his job, and his one night to bond with his aloof brother.

"Thank you," I said. "That was really good of you."

I spent the rest of the game glued to the table. As the game neared its end, I grabbed Eugene's arm.

"Let me take you to breakfast," I said. "I owe you that at least."

He shrugged and stepped out to smoke his neat joint.

"The Parker Meridien has the best breakfast in the city," he said when he came back.

"Wherever you want," I said.

I MADE $50,000 THAT NIGHT, which would solve a lot of my problems, but more importantly it had been a great game. Everyone seemed happy.

I was more surprised than anyone that I had made it work. As I walked out of the hotel, the sun was coming up. The city was still quiet. I hailed a cab and rode, beaming, to the Parker Meridien to meet Eugene. I was still astounded by his integrity. Without his help, my night would have turned out very differently.

He showed up a few minutes after I ordered a coffee.

"I just want to thank you again," I said.

"Are you going to thank me and then fire me?" he asked. He was smiling.

"No, the job of handing out chips is yours as long as you want it. You're welcome at any game I ever run."

We spent two hours at the restaurant. Beneath the street-punk facade, he was witty, clever, and intriguing. We talked about our families, relating to how lonely it was to be stuck in a sibling's shadow. Not only was Illya a prodigy poker player and gambler, which in his family was the skill that held the most value, he had also been a world-class tennis player.

Eugene told me a story that broke my heart and showed me where he fit into the family hierarchy. Over the previous summer, he had visited his brother in the Hamptons with his new pet kitten. Both Eugene and his pet had been bitten by a tick that carried Lyme disease, and had lain sick in bed together until the kitten died. With his family traveling for the summer and his brother rounding the games in Vegas, Eugene lay in bed, alone, forgotten. Half of his face became temporarily paralyzed and yet no one came to check on him. My heart hurt for him. His father didn't believe he could be a successful gambler due to the fact that he was "emotional." So Eugene dealt at a small game in Brooklyn and played with what he earned working the big game.

"Come work for me," I said. "You can deal my games. You'll make much more money."

"Kenneth won't let me."

"I'm starting other games. A lot of them."

"I'm in," Eugene said, and his dark eyes smiled at me from underneath his black hat.

KENNETH CALLED ME THE NEXT DAY.

"Most of the guys loved the game, but there are still a few who are hesitant. I suggested extending the trial period," he told me.

I was ecstatic. Given more time, I knew I could identify my critics and find a way to win them over.

A new schedule emerged from the ashes. Every week, the girls and I would fly to New York on Tuesday morning, arriving late in the afternoon, host the game that evening, stay up all night, and trudge, sleepless, to the airport the next day. I was also running a small game in L.A. that didn't pay as well as the one I had lost, but at least kept me attached to the scene. Over the weeks, Eugene and I became good friends, and he fed me important information. He told me that Keith Finkle was my most vocal critic. With awareness of what I had to overcome, I could plan accordingly.

New players with big bankrolls and a loose playing style were crucial to my status in New York. My NY game had a monstrous buy-in and enormous blinds, and these guys played for stakes most people had never heard of. This basically meant that anyone I brought in had to come loaded and ready to learn.

 196

But I was on a mission. I had something to prove, and I would not let my adversaries see me fail.

I ACTIVATED MY NETWORK, ran around town meeting with all of the wealthy friends and acquaintances I had ever met or known, and started spending more and more time in New York with my girls. I hired new recruits, brought some of my girls from L.A., and went out every night, cruising art-gallery openings, charity events, clubs, restaurants, happy hours.

Sunny was my dealer. She came with me from L.A. Sunny was a blond-haired, blue-eyed, free-spirited beauty. She looked the part of the inge-nue starlet but was much more interested in the poker tables and the DJ scene than in the silver screen. When she wasn't dealing, she was playing or dancing. She would frequently disappear for days and someone would have to finally physically remove her from the ratty L.A. casinos.

Lola was a sultry, dark-haired beauty who had grown up on Long Island, working and playing in local games. She was distractingly beautiful and a skilled player—a total secret weapon. When I needed to send a spy in to infiltrate a game, I could stake her. (Staking is the act of one person put-ting up cash for a poker player to play with, in hopes of the player winning. Any profits made are split on a predetermined percentage between the backer and the player.) And I knew that she would bring me new players and usually a nice profit.

Julia was gorgeous, Asian, and a math genius. Caroline's father was a diplomat, and she was a socialite who spoke five languages. Kendall was an all-American, corn-fed, blond, blue-eyed, girl-next-door type who was also a professional masseuse. Rider had a real knack for detective work, useful for when I needed help gathering intelligence to vet potential play-ers. Tiffany came with me from L.A. She was my playmate friend—a mas-ter seductress. Last, there was "Little," who was a five-foot-ten, blond, willowy model who excelled in organization and all things domestic; she was my personal assistant.

It was quite the crew, and I felt ready to take over the Big Apple. I moved and got a chic, modern apartment in Manhattan, with floor to ceil-ing windows, a great view, and plenty of room for the girls to crash.

I reached out to club promoters, bottle-service girls, "gallerinas" (beautiful girls hired by art galleries), and Atlantic City casino hosts, and offered them all cash incentives to send me players.

Quickly we became well-known around town. Mystique and allure followed us, whispers trailed behind us. Within a month, we were running the big game, which I rotated between the Four Seasons and the Plaza, and two smaller games that I ran out of my apartment. Luckily, my only neighbors on the floor were an NBA basketball player who was frequently gone and a semi-famous screenwriter who ironically loved poker and joined the game. The doormen, however, were very confused at first. Twice a week, nine to ten men and a crew of beautiful girls came over at 7 P.M. and didn't leave until the early morning hours.

Eventually, when I had given those doormen enough in tips to pay their rent, I told them what was going on. We had a good laugh about it.

THERE WAS, THOUGH, STILL TROUBLE BREWING in the form of Eddie Ting. Word traveled fast in the New York poker scene, and my games were quickly becoming infamous. Eddie had been displeased when I was thinking about setting up shop in New York . . . but now that I was here and had multiple games with many players, I was hearing more about him, and his feelings toward me, from lots of different people.

Eddie had approached Illya and asked him to stop me from running the big game; lucky for me, his influence was not as great as he wished. Of course, Eddie was upset. He had been shut out of the L.A. games and now his town was being overrun by a girl who didn't even play poker.

One evening, I got a tip that Arthur Grossman was in town. I had spies and informants all over the city, from club promoters to the aforementioned bottle-service girls to concierges at hotels. I was, by now, firmly grafted to NYC and I was making double, if not triple, what I made in L.A. I ran the games and everybody knew it; no one would dare disrespect me, or demand that I bark for tips. But I still had unfinished business. I wanted Arthur to look me in the eyes and tell me why he had cut me out. I had a feeling there was more to the story.

So, I sent him a text.

Hey Arthur, heard you're in town. I'm going out with the girls, would love to meet up.

He responded instantly. People respond so much more readily when you make an offer as opposed to a request.

We arranged to meet at Butter, a club down the street from my apartment and a notorious celeb hotspot. I called my friend, the owner of the club, and reserved the best table. As we all got ready, we drank champagne, laughed, did each other's makeup, and tried on different outfits. It was a typical girls'-night-out primping session . . . that is, until our runner, Little, arrived and laid stacks of cash out on the bed. She had been running around town doing collections from the big game.

We paused in our preparations to go through the stacks and check the math.

"Two-fifty," said Tiffany, presenting her stack.

"Three-forty," announced Kendall. We all looked at her. Math wasn't her strong suit.

"I counted it three times," she insisted.

"Two-eighty," said Julia, grabbing Kendall's stack to double-check.

"I've got four hundred thousand here," I said.

"Nice work, Little," I said, handing her a couple hundreds and a glass of champagne. "Catch up." I winked.

I put the money in the safe and put the finishing touches on my makeup.

GLIDING PAST THE LINE, we air-kissed the host and were escorted to our table, where Arthur was already waiting with his entourage. His eyes darted around quickly, taking in the bevy of beautiful girls.

I was charming, sweet, like nothing had ever happened. We drank and we danced, and I waited for my moment. Just then one of his assistants grabbed my arm, visibly drunk.

"I am so sorry about what happened in L.A.," she whispered into my ear. Her breath was hot and boozy on my cheek, and I wanted to pull away, but this was what I'd come for.

"You must be so upset. Why did he want you out so bad?" she slurred.

I looked at her.

"I didn't know that Arthur hated me so much," I said.

"No, not Arthur," she said. "Not Arthur. Tobey. It was all Tobey. I heard them talking. Arthur was worried about you."

I sat back in my seat, reeling. I had known that Tobey couldn't stand the money I was making, but I hadn't realized how deep the vein of his resentment went. If what Arthur's assistant told me was true, he used his celebrity to bait Arthur, and Arthur's money to bait the rest of the players, and then he pretended to be my friend so that he could deliver the parting blow.

I felt bitter, but I also marveled at how smart he was. I should have known.

I didn't say a word about the game to Arthur, just drank my scotch slowly and pretended to have fun.

At the end of the evening, Arthur took my arm.

"Come out to L.A.," he said. "Run a game at my house."

And just like that, I realized I could have L.A. back. Did I want it? I sure as hell wanted to look Tobey in the face, and I wanted it to be on my terms. So I agreed.

"Thanks, Arthur, I would love that," I said.

I HAD FANTASIZED ABOUT THIS MOMENT so many times since I lost my game . . . how they would come crawling back to me and beg me to return. It wasn't quite that dramatic, but it was enough to make me feel better—I would have been lying if I said I wasn't eager to see the look on Tobey's face when I showed up at the game from which he had engineered my ousting.

But before I could return to L.A., I had a little problem to deal with. One of the new players I had recruited, a guy named Will Fester, still hadn't paid the game, and he owed half a million. It had been three weeks and things weren't looking good.

I had only dealt with one stiff before, a professional athlete who, after the fact, I learned had some serious gang associations.

Back then, one of my players, a hip-hop producer, had offered to take care of the problem for me. He pulled me aside after the game.

"Yo, Molly, I could get you the dough from that scumbag."

"Really? How?"

"You don't want to ask that question."

I politely rejected the offer.

Covering the $40,000 that time was annoying, but it was a lot better than being involved in extortion or violence.

This time, finally, a mutual friend offered to reach out to my New York stiff. This friend was a very powerful man, worth several billion from his family's business. Will was in the same business, and I hoped that a call from our friend would be effective, since my voice mails had not been.

A day later, I finally got a call from Will.

"Hi, doll," he said.

"Hi, Will," I said, maintaining a friendly demeanor. It's too easy for guys not to pay if they become offended or angry.

"Sorry for the delay," he said. "It's been a crazy couple months. Can you meet me in Miami? I have cash down there and I don't want my wife to see this amount going out of my account."

"Sure."

"Tomorrow?"

"Just tell me where and when," I said. I held my breath until I heard back from him. I needed this guy to pay. The future of my NYC game depended on it.

Thankfully he texted me a place to meet and then I hung up and logged online to book a flight. I was about to click on purchase when it hit me: there was no way I could safely carry half a million in cash through Miami International Airport, the epicenter of drug trafficking. They kept closer watch there than at any airport in America.

I would have to charter a plane on the way home.

EUGENE OFFERED TO COME ALONG with me to make the pickup, so I booked a hotel room so that we could make it into a weekend. Eugene and I had quickly become involved. Our relationship evolved fast and furious, a heady experience and a very different kind of love affair from the one I'd had with Drew. Eugene knew my world. He had grown up in it. I never had to apologize for being stuck at work, or hide parts of what I did from him. Our love was open and honest, and for a time, it felt perfect.

When we landed in Miami, I texted Will. No response. I waited for an hour or two on pins and needles.

Would he really have me fly down here and be a no-show?

I was on the hook not only for his debt, but now for the plane I had chartered. I paced around nervously.

"Zil, it's gonna be okay," Eugene said. "Zilla" was his pet name for me. It was so nice to be with someone who understood everything I was going through. I had never experienced that since poker became my life.

Will finally showed up.

"I'm really sorry, Molly, it's been a tough couple months, the market and all."

I nodded sympathetically even though I knew from my casino sources that Will was regularly in Atlantic City and Vegas gambling huge numbers, despite the "market."

He tossed me a bag of cash, casino chips, and a gold bar. I counted the contents. He was still $100,000 short.

"I'll take care of the rest when I'm back in New York," he said, with an "I'll do better" face on.

I felt like yelling at him and telling him exactly what I thought of his degenerate ways but I needed to keep it amicable, at least until I collected the last $100,000.

He left and I turned to Eugene.

"Zil, if someone is going to stiff, they don't pay most of it, they stiff for the whole amount."

It made sense, it was logical. Eugene knew so much more about this world than I ever would. He had grown up around gamblers—it was almost part of his DNA. I had been spoiled in L.A., where no one stiffed because of the social consequences of the game. It was basically the same players in every game, and no one wanted to be blacklisted. I had a whole new roster in New York, and clearly a whole new set of rules to learn.

I had booked a room at the Setai, my favorite hotel on South Beach. I was excited to go to nice dinners with Eugene, lie on the sand, and relax with him. But Eugene was my little vampire, and he was in a heated, heads-up poker match online, so we ordered room service instead. He stayed up playing all night and didn't come to bed until around seven in the morning.

"I hate the sun anyway, Zil," he said, with sleep in his voice, as I got up to spend the day at the beach.

The second night, I staked Eugene in a local game. Supposedly, this was the biggest game in Miami and it was full of fish. He returned an hour before our 8 A.M. flight with a stack of cash and some valuable contacts.

It was a far cry from any trip I had been on with past boyfriends, but when we boarded our G-5 with a half a million in cash and gold bars, it felt pretty damn sexy, kind of like Bonnie and Clyde without the bloodshed.

Eugene stared at me with his black eyes as we buckled up.

"I love you so much," he said.

And I loved him too. More intensely than anyone I had ever been with. We used our love and our obsession with gambling to fill the voids of our lives, to insulate us from the reality we were both trying so hard to escape.

VEGAS WAS CALLING AGAIN. Illya had been on an extended stay and I needed him back in New York for the big game. He was notoriously afraid of flying, famous for "getting stuck" in places for months on end because he was too scared to get back on a plane. So I decided to multitask. I would orchestrate a Vegas trip, scoop Illya up, and bring the New York guys to L.A. to play in the game I was planning for Arthur.

I extended the invitations, chartered the jets, booked the hotels in Vegas and L.A., and planned an active social schedule. I brought Eugene along, of course. To everyone else he was just my employee. We did an immaculate job of hiding our relationship. Somehow it all came together and we boarded the jet in New York for Vegas. True to form, there wasn't a second between takeoff and landing when the guys weren't gambling on something. The plane ride consisted of a monster game of backgammon, Chinese poker, and a $500,000 freeze-out game between Russian Igor and the "Great Boudini," John Hanson, a mentor and business associate of Illya's. John, who had been one of the youngest chess masters in history, was like a human computer. He and Illya were always engaged in some heated discussion about stats and odds, Chinese poker, Hold'em, and stud.

Before we made ground in Vegas, there were already million-dollar figures in play.

THE RHYTHM INTRODUCED ON THE PLANE RIDE continued at the hotel. I hadn't even unpacked my bags in our sprawling and luxurious villa when the guys launched into a million-dollar game of Cee-lo, a dice game. Some were laying bets on sports. Some were reaching for the card decks, placing enormous sums on black or red.

I was following them around with my clipboard, frantically trying to keep track of everyone's figures. Every couple hours someone would call out for me, and I would have to calculate their net wins or losses.

"What's my number?"

"What's my number?"

It was madness. They played poker for a while, and then Phil Ivey, argu- ably the Tiger Woods of poker and one of the biggest gamblers in the world, asked me if *I* was feeling lucky. He wanted to play craps. We left the room and went to the tables, where I watched Ivey lose $3 million in a half hour.

It was day one, and the damage already exceeded $5 million.

We went to the clubs that night. A lot of the New York guys, rich as they were, were unaccustomed to this kind of access to the elite social scene I could provide. These were kings of the financial world, but they spent their days in suits, among other suits for the most part. I watched their faces, watched their body language, and the inherent value of decadence was evident. Selling the lifestyle had always been a powerful part of my pitch. No matter who the player was, if they had the money to play and pay, I could provide access to the most exclusive parties, beautiful women, celebrities, and billionaires . . . and the New York guys were much easier to impress than the L.A. ones. Eugene snuck into my room at night and whispered not only sweet words but intel and observations. He made ev- erything okay.

The next day, there was a game of golf for $100,000 a hole, another million-dollar buy-in poker game, another million-dollar Cee-lo game, and blackjack for $30,000 a hand.

By the time we left for L.A., the wins and losses were well into eight digits. No one had slept; all the men were completely manic. As we left Vegas and headed to the private airport in Los Angeles, monstrous back- gammon and Chinese poker games were going on in full force before the pilots closed the doors. I fought to keep my eyes open but I couldn't miss recording a win or loss.

I watched and I couldn't help but wonder if things were getting dan- gerously out of control. These guys were mainlining gambling like a drug. Nothing was ever enough. The wins multiplied, but they never covered the losses. This just created more compulsion. These men could afford it, and this was what they chose to do for pleasure. It wasn't hurting anyone. At least this is what I told myself.

Chapter 27

*D*espite the decimated economy, the resistance from my New York competitors like Eddie Ting, and the perception that I had been forced to leave L.A. to save face after losing everything, the reality was that I had won. And I had won spectacularly. My New York games were bigger, better, and more profitable than the Los Angeles game had been. I had a much different perspective now, though, with the memory of what I had gone through never far from my mind. I wouldn't allow myself to become complacent; I never stopped searching for the next whale, the next donkey. Eugene had become an integral part of that. I made him a partner and vogued for him constantly so he could play in games that might garner contacts. My vogue was as good as gold and it enabled him to play in every game in the city. We still kept the romantic part of our relationship under wraps. This arrangement was hugely beneficial to me in a business sense, but I lost him to the night. For the first time in his life, Eugene had carte blanche to gamble anywhere and everywhere and I realized why his father had given Illya, not him, the backpack of cash to infiltrate New York. Eugene was an addict. He would sometimes play for two days straight. He was quickly becoming one of the biggest fish in New York City. And unfortunately, when he stayed at a game too long, he would start to get emotional when he lost and the tilt would start. All of his hard-earned knowledge and strategy would go out the window. As much as he was recruiting valuable players and gathering important intelligence for me, he was also running up quite a debt. I barely saw him anymore.

MY WEALTHY FRIENDS GAVE ME lots of great leads; one in particular led me to Glen Reynolds. Allegedly, Glen was young, rich, and reckless. A mutual friend connected us and we started communicating by phone and e-mail. I invited him to a few games. He was definitely interested, as evidenced by all of the questions he asked, but he didn't show up right away. Glen had a habit of calling the day after a game and wanting to know the gossip and the results. I was happy to oblige . . . I was baiting the hook.

Glen finally appeared at nine o'clock on a Friday night when I was doing an experimental game with smaller stakes, with a buy-in of only $5,000.

I had all the girls working, dressed to the nines and drinking to loosen up the mood. I was hoping that by lowering the stakes and creating a party atmosphere, I could build a fun game that felt less serious than the big game. Eugene had brought along some of the biggest fish he had met and I filled the table with the rest of my recruits.

Glen took one look at me when he walked in, and in his Long Island accent with all of the aggression and fervor of a trader, exclaimed, "What the fuck are you doing running poker games? You should be barefoot and pregnant, doing yoga or shopping."

His comment surprised me, but so did my reaction. I was offended, but my stomach also did a little somersault. It was the first time in a while that a man had spoken to me like I was a woman. He wasn't exactly good-looking, but there was something about him that was attractive, while also simultaneously offensive.

Out of the corner of my eye I saw Eugene watching us.

Glen ordered a Red Bull and vodka, downed it in two seconds, and told Tiffany to keep them coming. Then he handed her a hundred-dollar chip.

He was exactly who I wanted him to be.

At the beginning of the night the game was exactly as I had hoped—friendly and social. But after Glen had a couple cocktails he started driving the action up. Soon he was in for $100,000 and the rest of the guys smelled blood in the water, and that was the end of my friendly game.

THERE'S SOMETHING THAT HAPPENS to people when they see the opportunity to make money. Greed flavored with desperation, especially at a poker table, gives rise to a moment when the eyes change, the humanity vanishes, and the players become bloodthirsty, flat-eyed predators.

The first time I really saw this play out was in L.A. when Ned Berkley, the bad-boy heir to his family's company, came to play. It was very obvious that Ned didn't exactly know the rules of poker. The guys sensed it immediately, flipped into greed mode, and turned into a hungry pack, and by the end of the night, Ned had lost a small fortune.

The pack wasn't done with him, though. They were drunk with greed. They asked Ned what he liked to play.

"Blackjack," he said, not wanting to disappoint his new celebrity friends. Not surprisingly, he was also a terrible blackjack player. The guys took turns playing the house. I could see them dealing cards as fast as they could. Nodding and whispering to each other.

Their greed was so transparent that I cringed as I watched Ned's face register what was going on. He tried to quit but they egged him on. He continued to play, lost graciously, and paid, but I knew he would never come back.

GLEN APPROACHED, holding another Red Bull and vodka and wanting another $100,000.

"Come talk to me first."

We walked into my bedroom, where he made himself comfortable on my bed.

"Nice room," he said, waving his arm at the floor-to-ceiling windows.

"Thanks. So, I usually ask first-time players to post. I'm on the hook for the cash, as you know. Where's your head?"

I was only a little worried. Number one, my friend had vouched for this guy; number two, his ego was clearly life-size and his peers were at the table. Three, I had word from Vegas that he had won a million last month.

But . . . he was drunk and getting killed.

"I'm good for it. You have nothing to worry about." Then he said, "Tell me about you . . . I'm fascinated."

I smiled but didn't respond.

"Okay, well. If you won't tell me, then I guess I'll go back to the table."

We looked at each other, and there was undeniable chemistry.

I got up and walked out, and I could feel him close behind. Eugene stared intently at us as we walked out of my room. I smiled reassuringly at him.

It was 3 A.M. and some of the more responsible guys were getting up.

Keith Finkle, one of the hedge-fund guys from my big game proposed they play stud. Glen enthusiastically agreed.

Oh no, I thought. This was bad. Hold'em was one thing, but stud was a bigger game with much more risk, and Keith was by far the best player I had ever seen.

Meanwhile, I was getting calls from players from my other games— Illya, Eugene's brother, and Helly Nahmad, both wanting to confirm that Glen was on tilt and bleeding money. I confirmed.

Helly and Illya had been coming around more often lately, even to my smaller games. I heard they had put together a sports betting group that allegedly included John Hanson, the brilliant chess master, a kid from MIT who had developed an algorithm for picking winning teams, and an IT programmer-type genius to keep track of it all.

They both showed up and bought in for a hundred grand, and Keith added chips as well.

Suddenly my little $5,000 Texas Hold'em game had become a $100,000 buy-in stud game.

As the sun came up, the girls and I scurried around dropping the black-out blinds and ordering breakfast and coffee for everyone . . . except Glen, who was on his thousandth Red Bull with vodka.

My staff and I were exhausted but the game was crazy good and all the girls were cleaning up in tips. Glen was in for $400,000, so we ordered lunch, more cigarettes, and more vodka. We put on the sports channels for the guys: I had several television screens in my living room for this very purpose. But I was close to cutting Glen off because I couldn't afford a hit this big if he decided not to pay.

Most game runners are essentially running Ponzi schemes. They extend massive credit without actually having the capital to back it up: that's why most games die. I didn't work this way—I didn't extend credit I couldn't back up, and I always covered. I couldn't afford to die.

Luckily, Glen started winning somehow. He smiled and winked at me, and again, his flirtation affected me. There was something about his reck-lessness that was a turn-on. I looked at Eugene, and though I still loved him, I knew the limitations. He could never be a real boyfriend if I ever left this world.

GLEN AND KEITH WERE IN A HUGE HAND, and when it went Glen's way, it was a huge win for him. Keith bought $300,000. Glen was counting his chips.

"Can I take three hundred K in chips off the table?" he asked. I looked at Keith. It was essentially up to the table to allow a player to put some of his winnings aside this way, because the rules said no. In a no-limit game, all money stays in play.

I motioned to Keith to indicate that the decision was his to make, and predictably, he refused, so they kept playing. It was now 4 P.M. They had been playing for nearly a full day. I sent the girls home and brought in a new shift of dealers. Glen then lost a monster hand to Illya. Soon, maybe the exhaustion or the Red Bull caught up with him and he went on major tilt, and wiped out his whole stack.

I watched him buy in for $50,000. When a losing player starts buying small in a big game, it usually means they will continue to lose.

He lost it and stood up.

"I'm done."

He went to use the bathroom. The guys surrounded me instantly.

"Is he good for it?"

"Will he come back?"

"Can I get paid first?"

I was exhausted and annoyed.

Glen came back and motioned for me to speak in private with him.

"Hey," he said. "I have three hundred and fifty K in cash at my house. I won it in Vegas last month."

I nodded, feigning surprise.

"I can get it to you now or tomorrow," he said.

"Now is great," I said.

As I was getting ready to leave, Eugene grabbed my arm.

"You okay? Want me to come?"

"I'm good, see you in a few," I said

This was another of my rules: You don't ever let a gambler sleep on a debt if you can help it. You don't want them to have time to lose it, or think too much about it and decide to stiff.

Helly valiantly offered his white Phantom and driver for my collections mission, and Glen and I enjoyed an awkward ride together in the back of the ostentatious car. We were both exhausted and he was nursing a wounded ego. But there was still an undeniable sexual tension between us.

We rode up the elevator in a strange silence. He went back to get the money from the safe and handed it to me in an envelope. I stuck it in my purse.

"Thanks," I said.

"I'll call you tomorrow," said Glen, and reached out to hug me.

Startled, I tipped off balance and he caught me, holding me for a moment longer than he needed to before he settled me back on my feet. I was staring straight into his eyes and I felt like he was going to kiss me.

"You must be exhausted," I said, and the moment passed.

"Yeah," he said, but he was still staring at me intensely.

"Good night," I said. The sun was out and it was the middle of the afternoon.

"'Night," he said.

I counted the bills on the way back to the apartment, and it was all there. When I walked in, the vultures were waiting.

"Did you get it?"

"Do you have it?"

"Yeah," I said. "We'll deal with it in the morning. I have some things to figure out."

"Can I just get a hundred K?" asked Helly.

"I'll call you tomorrow," I said, and went into my room.

There was a knock on the door. I opened it and Helly was standing there with a look on his face.

"Can I just have ten K? I owe my bookie."

I sighed and handed him the money, then shut the door firmly and lay down to get some rest. Eugene came in a few moments later and curled up next to me. For the first time in a long time we were on the same sleep schedule and I remembered how nice it was to not be alone.

I WOKE UP TO A MESSAGE from Glen that said: *I'm contesting the other 150. You should have let me take 300K off the table.*

I groaned and buried my face in the pillow.

The game needed to be paid out, and I had guaranteed it. If someone didn't pay, I would have to write the check. I knew Glen didn't have a strong argument—or any argument at all—but in this world that didn't matter. There weren't any courts, judges, contracts, or police officers.

Most game runners, when they got stiffed, behaved like gangsters; they sold the debts on the streets or hired muscle and tried to intimidate people into paying—or worse. That just wasn't an option for me: I may have been operating in the gray but I still had a moral system and awareness (or so I thought) of the law, and intimidation and violence crossed both lines. My only line of defense was my understanding of human behavior and my problem-solving skills. I knew there was a solution; I just had to be smart enough to get there.

After observing Glen for more than twenty-four hours, what I knew about him was the following: he had a huge ego, he was affected by pretty girls and seemed to want to impress them, he had a ton of gamble in him, he was an alpha male, and he had the money to pay. Based on the information at hand, I knew I couldn't push him, and I couldn't be threatening or appear angry. I just needed to provide compelling upside for him to pay his debt.

The two most valuable assets in this debt collection were incentive, specifically access to beautiful girls, great games, and important people, and my femininity. If I could get him to view me as a woman whom he could save by simply paying his debt, I had a much better chance of collecting.

I picked up the phone and called him. He answered gruffly, already preparing for a collection call in which he would stand his ground and maintain his position that the floor call had been unfair.

"Hiiii, whatcha up to tonight?" I asked lightly.

"Nothing," he said, still stiff.

"Come to dinner and the club with the girls and me."

He paused. I needed him to say yes. Getting "social" with him was a hugely important part of my plan.

"Who's coming?"

I listed their names.

"Okay," he said. "What time?"

GLEN WAS PROMPT, and visibly pleased to be the only guy surrounded by seven girls who were doting on him and laughing at his jokes. Not a word was mentioned about his debt that night.

When the bill came, he made a big, ceremonious show of picking up the tab. I smiled and thanked him profusely. Inside I was laughing. He still owed me $150,000, so his attempt at chivalry fell about $149,000 short.

We went on to a club, where the promoter gave us our usual welcome and escorted us to one of the best tables. The alcohol flowed, the girls danced, Glen kept looking happy. He came to sit next to me on the banquette. I was doing figures (the math of debts and collections) on my phone.

"Hi," he said. "How come you're sitting here by yourself and not having fun like everyone else?"

I gave him a brave smile.

"I'm just a little stressed, trying to solve some problems."

"You're too pretty to have problems."

"I came here after losing everything in L.A. and I really need this to work. I have mouths to feed," I said motioning to the girls, "and something to prove."

"I get it," he said, looking into my eyes. "We'll figure it out. Now come have fun. It'll be okay, I promise."

Bingo.

Two weeks later, Glen showed up to my big game with a check for the $150,000. That night he won $300,000, so I ripped the check.

He quickly became one of my most valuable players.

I rarely saw Eugene anymore. He played in the day games, the night games. He was gone for days—he would come home and crawl into bed and sleep for twenty-four hours and then leave again. He wasn't recruiting much anymore, and although he didn't do it intentionally, he was supporting my competitors.

Chapter 28

I decided to get a house in the Hamptons for the summer. It was too hot in the city, and most of the players were out on the island for the summer anyway, so I hired a real-estate agent and found a sprawling mansion with impeccable grounds, an infinity pool, and a tennis court that came with a tennis instructor for the summer. The house was so big that the girls and I had our own wing. Strategically, I had arranged to share the house with Illya and Keith. This would almost certainly ensure plenty of games and gambling at the house, and I could offset the pricey rent.

ON FRIDAY, the girls and I piled into my Bentley and headed east for the first weekend of the summer. We had a full social schedule planned—fashion shows, a new restaurant opening, and, of course, the annual Bridgehampton Polo Match, the official kickoff of the summer social season. We arrived in the late afternoon and the girls squealed with excitement when they saw the sprawling estate. Everyone raced upstairs to claim rooms and start getting ready.

I made myself comfortable out by the large saltwater pool, dressed in a white dress, and began drinking rosé.

The heaviness of my life had lifted and for the moment I had peace. My heart had that full feeling that only comes when everything in the world is right again.

The Bridgehampton Polo Match was only attended by the who's who of high society. Impeccably dressed socialites holding flutes of champagne in manicured hands, distinguished-looking gentlemen reeking of old money, A-list celebrities, and impossibly beautiful models congregated under the white tents, while handsome equestrians like Nacho Figueras warmed up on the lush green fields. It was easy to get lost in the novelty and glamour of it all, but I was there for a purpose. I knew this would be fertile ground for recruiting players. The girls and I found a table and sipped our champagne while taking in the scene. We were new faces on the circuit and it didn't take long for a steady stream of men to approach the table. By now we were pros at subtly but quickly determining whether or not a guy was a potential player.

I was entertaining a pharmaceutical-company billionaire when I looked up and saw Glen with his arm around a pretty blonde. To my utter annoyance I felt a pang of jealousy. Eugene was my soul mate and I loved him in a way I hadn't known I was capable of, but he was disappearing more each day. Glen was arrogant and self-absorbed. He looked over and we made eye contact, I smiled and quickly looked away. It was just as well. Nothing, absolutely nothing, good could come of dating Glen Reynolds.

That night, we had a party at our house, and I continued what I had started at the polo event, working the crowd looking for assets/players. By the time I crawled into bed, I was exhausted but thrilled by the amount of contacts we had obtained.

I wanted to call Eugene and tell him how well things were going, so I dialed his number. It went straight to voice mail, as usual. I thought about him dressed in black, going from game to game, not sleeping for days, and finally crashing in his gilded apartment in Trump Tower, alone. It made my heart hurt. And then I checked one last time to see if the awful Glen Reynolds had texted. He hadn't.

When Glen called me a few days later to ask me to dinner, I politely declined. But he wasn't one to give up. He asked again and again, and I always said no.

AND THEN HE GOT SMART; Glen knew the way to my heart was through my game.

A week or two later, he sent me a text asking if I would do a game at his house in the city, saying that his Wall Street buddies wanted to play.

I couldn't say no. Glen had offered to bring new players. I showed up at his place with the girls, my dealers, my table, Shuffle Master, chairs, snacks, and an intention to be all business.

"Sweetheart . . ." he said when he opened the front door, giving me his most charming smile. He folded me in a very tight hug. I patted his shoulder politely and wiggled out of his embrace.

"Where should we set up?" I asked, trying to stay focused.

He led me into his living room. His apartment was nice but it was definitely a bachelor's pad. As his friends showed up, he introduced me. They were all young, rich, fast-talking Wall Street guys.

It didn't take long for the game to get crazy. The energy was great; these guys gambled in the market all day and seemed to ride out the swings easily. I started getting calls from players asking for seats.

I sent Glen a text regarding the last seat, mentioning that I had a lot of good options.

I have one more guy coming, he wrote.

The doorbell rang. I went to open the door expecting to see another slick-suited trader and instead found myself face-to-face with Eddie Ting.

I looked back at Glen and he nodded.

"Hi, Molly," Eddie said in a very friendly voice.

"Hi," I said, trying to hide my anger. I was now very annoyed with Glen. How could he ask me to run a game and leave out the fact that my archenemy and biggest competition would be showing up?

"Need to talk," I whispered in Glen's ear after I set Eddie up with chips. We went into the den.

"What are you doing! He is going to steal the players. This is my livelihood, this is my business," I explained to him in a heated tone.

"I've known Eddie for years; he wanted to play and he wants to make nice with you. I promise you," he said, putting his hands on my shoulders and looking sincerely into my eyes, "nobody is stealing anything from you, I'll make sure of it."

Of course, Eddie wanted to make nice with me now. I had the best games in New York. I had access to players that he did not. I knew what he was up to.

The game went smoothly, and I played it very cool with Glen, keeping it strictly business despite his obvious attempts at flirtation.

He came to find me in the kitchen.

"Are you mad at me about the girl I brought to the polo match or about the Eddie Ting thing?"

"Mad? Who's mad?" I said lightly.

"You scare me," he said.

"I doubt that," I said, refreshing his drink. "You don't seem the scared type."

"Will you let me drive you to the Hamptons this weekend?"

"I don't think that would be a good idea," I said.

"Oh, relax, I'm not trying to sleep with you. I want to talk to you about something."

He saw my skepticism. "It's business-related."

Say no, Molly, say no, say no.

It was one of those moments when you have a clear choice to go down the right path or the wrong. I knew exactly how this story would end. I knew it had a high potential to be detrimental to my game. But I missed Eugene so much sometimes that it hurt physically, and the attention from Glen was at least a temporary distraction.

"Fine," I said, ignoring my internal radar. "But it better really be about business."

I knew full well that it was not.

I ALSO KNEW I NEEDED to end things with Eugene. Eugene was gone. I loved him but he didn't fit into my world anymore. I wanted to try to have a real boyfriend, not a boy who lived in the shadows. I texted him; I was afraid if I saw him I wouldn't be able to do it. I tried to be pragmatic, I told him it wasn't working out. We never saw each other. He should do his thing, he was young, and I needed more. We could still be business partners and always best friends.

He showed up at my door in the pouring rain. He stood there, soaking wet, his eyes dark pools of pain. I pulled him inside and we held each other and cried. My heart felt like it was being ripped from my chest. His tears made me sadder than anything I could remember.

"Why, Zilla?" he asked. "I love you so much. I would never hurt you like this."

His pain brought me to my knees, but I turned my head and choked back a sob. "It's just not working. We will always be friends and business partners."

He pressed his tear-soaked face against mine; he put his hands on my face and kissed me hard. I could feel his tears and his mouth—passionate and heartbroken. I pressed against him; I didn't know how I could possibly survive without him. Emptiness flooded my chest.

He looked into my eyes . . . and then he left.

"I'll always love you, Zil, always."

I closed my eyes and listened to him leave.

Love was a liability. I just couldn't allow it into my world. I pushed the pain and the emptiness somewhere into the back of my mind and packed my bags for the weekend.

GLEN PICKED ME UP IN HIS BLACK BMW.

"I like you," he said, looking intensely into my eyes.

"You don't know me," I said. "I'm definitely not your type."

"What's my type?" he asked. He was laughing.

"Barefoot and pregnant," I shot back, referring to his comment the first time we met.

"We can work on that." He was still laughing.

"You will never be able to handle my life, my job."

"I'll handle it. I like it. I think it's cool that you're so ambitious."

I knew he wouldn't think it was very cool when it took me from his bed five nights a week, or when he wasn't invited out on recruiting nights, or on trips. In the past I wouldn't have given Glen a second look. I would have stayed focused, but somewhere inside I was beginning to want something more than this life.

In the beginning, dating Glen was great. We went on normal dates to great restaurants, he took me to plays and charity events. I still loved Eugene. I thought of him often and wondered when the pain in my heart would subside, but I was able to have an adult relationship with Glen, and that was nice. The game I hosted at his house was profitable and entertaining. Eddie showed up every week, going out of his way to be my friend.

In my gut I knew not to trust Eddie, but he was growing on me. He was funny and self-deprecating and he seemed to have abandoned all ill will. Before too long, I relaxed my defenses. To my surprise we became friends, actual friends.

Our cease-fire proved advantageous. There was an unspoken bond that came from a shared experience . . . Eddie and I were the biggest game runners in the world and we understood each other in a way that nobody else could. He came to play at my games with his most valuable players and I sent him some as well. We formed a united front to people who owed us money, and helped each other collect. If a guy who owed Eddie money won in my game, I would transfer the winning to Eddie instead of paying the winner, and he did the same for me.

We began to socialize too, Glen and me double-dating with Eddie and his wife.

Life was good. Glen and I were having fun, most of my games were great, and I didn't feel the imminent threat of enemies, either overt or subversive. Still, though, cracks were starting to appear.

I still thought about Eugene. He fell deeper and deeper into the black hole. He was playing in every game, even the shadier games in Brooklyn and Long Island. He was running up huge debts. Last I heard he had been fooled into paying half a million to become a partner in a rival game. I tried to reason with him.

"Eugene, you are the asset. Not only do you bring players, you play for days, creating enough action that everyone stays and runs the rake sky-high," I'd tell him whenever we had a few encounters, mostly financial transactions. I knew the door to our private world had disappeared.

I was also starting to have some issues filling the big game. I lost a few players—one to an ultimatum from his new, young, and gorgeous second wife, and another to a guy unraveling over a Madoff investment. It wasn't the end of the world to skip the big game a couple of weeks, but it left me open to be pushed out. I wasn't about to let this one go. It was too lucrative, too big.

I was talking to Eddie. "Kenneth is just a gold mine. What you have built is so impressive; you can always build a game around Kenneth," he'd tell me.

"It's getting harder than you would think," I said. "I think even the gods of Wall Street are coming down a bit from their untouchable thrones."

"Why don't we partner on the game?" Eddie offered casually. "I can supplement the players you are losing, and I'll play." He had one huge whale and a whole stable of players whom he had staked throughout the years.

"Yeah, that may work, let me think about it . . ."

"Sweet," he said, and poured me a shot of tequila. "We could be an unstoppable team."

I was so conflicted. On one hand, I wanted to trust Eddie, wanted to believe this wasn't a long con to steal my big game. On the other hand, it would be very, VERY nice to have someone to share the financial strain of covering the slow payers' debts and the stress of filling the seats. By this time I was bankrolling and guaranteeing the game. If a guy paid slowly or took more than a week, I wrote the check myself to ease the anxiety that the winner might feel.

Eddie and almost all the other game runners allow a pro or two in at their tables, and take a percentage of their wins and losses. The fact that I wasn't a player allowed me to be a lot more objective and fair about the game as a whole.

Against my better judgment I decided to give Eddie's proposal a try. He showed up with his finest assets in tow and a few pros. Kenneth was not happy. Eddie was the life of the party, though, the loosest action in the game. I knew this was not how he typically played and that it was the opportunity he had been waiting for. He had come a long way from the one-dollar, two-dollar rat holes. Kenneth won and the game was a huge success. I had let Eddie speak to the dealers about the rake. I had never raked the big game before. Mostly because there had been very little risk in the game, and the tips were enormous.

At the end of the night, after the players left, Eddie and I ran the numbers. Between the rake and our "horses" (guys we were taking a piece of), we each made over $200,000. That was much more than I had ever made in a game. I was energized by the huge profit, but I also felt a nagging guilt, as if I had cheated or stolen from my friends. It just felt dirty.

I was riding high. I had befriended my enemies, charmed my critics, and I was making so much money I couldn't even spend it.

GLEN, WHO HAD BEEN A DILETTANTE PLAYER before we met, was now playing regularly. He wanted to make the game at his house a weekly thing.

"It'll be your game and you can have total control," he said.

That was a problem. Having the game at a player's house detracted from my power. But I acquiesced. He was my boyfriend.

Glen was consistently the biggest loser. This presented another challenge, because my position as collector was now largely about collecting from my boyfriend and using that cash to pay his peers and my salary.

I also had other games to babysit, and ducking out of Glen's games wasn't easy. One particular evening, he was down $200,000 and I had to get to another game.

That night, there were a few loose cannons at Glen's game. One of them was Deacon Right a young trust-fund kid. Deacon was a bad player. Very bad.

Deacon loved to get Glen on tilt.

"Glen? Your girl is leaving?" he said.

And then he turned to me.

"You're leaving your man's game at midnight? Where could you be going?"

I gritted my teeth. It wasn't my "man's" game, first and foremost, because I had invited most of the players and I was guaranteeing the game. I was taking risks in order to make the game great—like letting Deacon play, for example.

Deacon kept going.

"Your girl is leaving and you're down two hundred K?" he pressed.

Glen shot me a nasty look. I had to get to the other game to check the books, the sheet, and the credit. The numbers had been off last week, and I was concerned because I thought my bookkeeping system was foolproof.

My personal life and my professional life were once again at odds, and I wasn't happy about it. In this room, at this game, I wasn't Glen's cheerleader or his girlfriend, I was running a business. If I left now, I would embarrass him in front of his friends, and I didn't want him to lose even more money, but I needed to take care of other business.

I got up to leave and he signaled to wait.

He came into the hall.

"It's midnight," he said.

"I need to check on the other game."

We argued for a minute, and I cut him off.

"I'm going. I'll be back later."

On the stairs, I turned back to say good night. He slammed the door in my face.

AS SOON AS I GOT TO THE OTHER GAME, Willy Engelbert, a rich New York City kid, rushed up to me with his stack.

"Another crazy comeback," he said breathlessly.

"Nice job," I said, looking at him closely. Something felt off. I had seen thousands of wins and losses and something wasn't right.

"Can I get paid?" he asked in the same breathy, desperate way.

Meanwhile, the host of the game was stuck for a huge number and had apparently convinced my assistant to give him much more credit than I would feel comfortable with. The host, although wealthy and supposedly a partner in the game, was too much of a degenerate to be trusted.

I was glad that I had come. It was like a free-for-all at this game. There were some unknown faces there who looked a little out of place, and the dealer had been working for three hours, at the host's insistence. I didn't like my dealers working for longer than an hour at a time.

It was time to gain control of the game. I had a talk with the host, who showed me his account balances online and even transferred some cash into my account. I then tried to get acquainted with the new faces as I straightened out the books.

Glen was blowing up my phone.

"Game's over, where the fuck are you? This is so unprofessional, I need you to settle the books and pay people."

I ran back into the cold night and hailed a cab back over to Glen's so I could balance the books there and write checks to the winners and the staff. According to my books, Glen had lost $210,000 and he was pissed. After he wrote the checks to the winners, he stomped off to his room.

I quietly snuck back out to the other game to make sure it was running smoothly. When I was finally satisfied that my staff had it under control, I went back over to Glen's just as the sun was coming up.

I crawled into bed praying I wouldn't wake him.

"I'm keeping the tips tonight, and I want to be figured in retroactively to all the games we have done," he said, his back to me.

Anger filled my chest like wildfire. I wanted to yell and scream all the reasons why this demand was so unfair, unjust, and unethical—like, for instance, the fact that he was a trader on Wall Street and this was my whole business.

I had spent my life building my business so I could play by my own rules and love someone for real and not because I needed them.

In that moment Glen became my enemy. So instead of arguing, I became calm. I needed to strategize.

"Let's talk about it later," I said, and rolled over, pretending to sleep until he left for work

I WOKE TO A 6 A.M. TEXT FROM MY DEALER.

Game was off by 10,000 again.

My mind flashed to Willy and how suspicious he had made me feel. And when I started looking closer, I discovered that last night's game wasn't the only one that had been off for the past couple of weeks.

I contacted the other game runners that Willy frequented, and they all confirmed that Willy had been at all the games linked to an accounting discrepancy.

Calling someone out as a cheater without concrete proof would cause a whole host of issues. Willy would simply deny it, say it was coincidence, and then possibly bad-mouth me around town. What I needed was proof. What I needed was to catch him red-handed. So I quietly had cameras installed, positioning them in a way that wouldn't compromise any of the other players by showing their hands or their faces.

The only way Willy could get away with this, I reasoned, was if he somehow added chips to his stack without buying in. It was possible that he had ordered custom chips that were identical to mine or was somehow stealing from my set or the chips on the table.

Sure enough, at the next game, when Willy, who was a terrible player, was down again—he somehow ended up with a small win. Then he practically begged to be paid immediately.

I watched the surveillance, and clear as day, throughout the game, he was sneaking chips from his pocket onto the table.

I called Willy and asked him to come by my apartment, telling him that I had all his checks ready.

He showed up, rosy-cheeked from the cold, and wearing a very expensive coat.

"Hi!" he said, giving me a kiss and a hug. "I just want you to know how awesome your games are, you run the best game in the city and everyone knows it."

I smiled and thanked him.

"I want to show you something."

He watched the tape and his face turned pale.

"Molly, you don't understand how much pressure I'm under," he said, sounding frantic.

"I got in some trouble with some bad people and I can't ask my family for help; they would kill me—they already think I'm a loser."

He was actually crying. I handed him some tissues.

"I understand," I lied. Poor rich kid who would rather steal than face his parents. He was a thief, a cheat, and a coward, but I needed him to see me as someone doing him a favor, not as a foe. Willy was desperate and unscrupulous, and that makes for a dangerous enemy. So I positioned myself as his ally.

"Listen, I won't show anyone this tape, but you have to pay back the games you stiffed, and you can't ever play again. I'm going to rip up these checks and you can pay me the balance when you are back on your feet. You play with a lot of your dad's friends and important people that may be instrumental to your future."

He agreed immediately, sounding grateful and apologizing repeatedly.

I knew that if I had confronted him without proof, he would have gotten nasty. I also knew that the other game runners in town would not have handled this so diplomatically.

"Pay your debts and the video is yours."

He gave me a hug before he left, looking humiliated and beaten.

"Thanks for handling it like this," he said quietly. "You're a good girl."

IN THE END, Willy paid me in full, and I gave him the tape. Obviously I kept a copy, but I never heard from him again and I never had to use it.

The fiasco taught me a valuable lesson: I couldn't ever let anyone else run my games. I had to be there.

ONE OF MY REGULAR PLAYERS called just after Willy left to contest a $250,000 sum that he had paid to Illya back in December.

This player currently owed the game around a million and he was basically telling me that he wouldn't be paying $250,000. I called Illya, who, of course, said the guy was wrong.

I closed my eyes and leaned my head back on the couch, exhausted in a way I had never been before. Sleepless and emotionally drained as I was, the weight of the responsibilities that rested solely on my shoulders were starting to feel physically crushing. To make matters worse, I had to go talk to Glen.

He answered the door and I paused, not knowing what kind of mood he would be in.

He hugged me close.

"I'm sorry, baby, I was out of line. You can have it all, the game, all of it."

I wanted to believe him, but I didn't. I was too tired to fight and I allowed myself to collapse into his arms. I longed for Eugene's goodness, the purity of his love.

I convinced myself I was helping Eugene, but I was helping myself and I felt guilt weighing heavily on my chest. I hadn't helped him, I ruined him.

Glen and I went to dinner that night and we both drank too much wine. He grabbed my hands as if he were going to propose to me.

"What's the number?"

"What do you mean?"

"What's the amount of money that would make you leave poker? I'll write the check. I'll invest in anything you do."

He took out his checkbook. His eyes were crazy.

"What is it? I'll write it right now!"

"Why? So you can own me?" I was suddenly furious. Glen was so used to being able to use his money to control situations. And now he was trying to use it to control me.

"There's no number, Glen. I can't be bought."

THINGS WITH GLEN GOT WORSE AND WORSE. He became more controlling, and I pulled away. The more I pulled back, the more I felt him trying to control me, and with the only effective means he had: the game.

According to my records, he never paid me the $210,000 he lost the night we'd first fought. He began withholding more money that I believe he owed when he lost at other games, telling me I was a bad girlfriend when I tried to collect.

When I finally checked into a hotel under an alias and wrote him a good-bye e-mail, he was devastated. He called me, my friends, my assistants. He came to the Plaza and demanded to know which room I was in. He lost his composure completely.

Somehow, I wasn't surprised.

THE NEXT DAY, I e-mailed Kenneth Redding about the big game. He responded immediately.

**We're playing tonight at Eddie's.
I thought you were doing it together.**

I felt the blood rush to my face. Fuck. Fuck. Fuck.

I knew instantly what was happening. Glen must have gone to Eddie and forced him to choose a side. And Eddie, who I had believed was my friend, was actually no one's friend. He was a businessman, and he saw his chance to cut me out and gain Glen as an asset.

I felt the rage exploding out of me. I picked up a glass and threw it hard at the wall. It shattered into a thousand pieces.

THE NEXT FEW WEEKS WERE HELL. Eddie had the big game, Glen was running my Monday-night game at his house, and I could barely get one game off a week. Neither Glen nor Eddie would return my calls. According to my records, they both owed me a lot of money.

If you're going to steal from me or go back on your word, at least have the courage to look me in the face.

My mind was reeling. I wouldn't just lie down and accept this fate. I wasn't going to run scared the way I had done in Los Angeles. Plus, this time I didn't have anywhere to go.

I started concocting schemes to get my game back. I had information that could ruin both of them. Of course I did. I knew everyone's secrets. I hosted their nights of transgressions. But they could ruin me right back. We were all exposed in some way. Some of us were breaking serious laws. And so I took the high road.

I had more contacts. I had other games. But the novelty of New York was wearing off.

Part Six

COLD DECK

New York, June 2010–2011

Cold Deck (noun)

A deck that has been intentionally rigged ("stacked") such that the player cannot win.

Chapter 29

Summer was here again, and the long cold winter, both actual and metaphorical, gave way to hope and hedonism. I rented another mansion in the Hamptons, and the girls and I geared up for parties, polo, and, of course, games.

I had rebuilt my roster, and I was making money again, but I wasn't enjoying it much. I was tired. Tired of being taken advantage of. It seemed that unless I was willing to stoop to their level, I couldn't compete with people who had no honor. I had to constantly watch my back, and it felt like everyone I met was trying to steal my games, and all my "friends" were on my payroll or players in the game. I was growing weary of the weight and the loneliness.

I spent July in Ibiza and Saint-Tropez doing what I had always done: recruiting, politicking, and playing. One night in Ibiza, I collected $50,000 from various people who owed me money; they all just handed me stacks of cash. But the passion and fervor were missing. Instead of dancing on the tables with the rest of them, I sat at a banquette and watched the swirl of half-naked girls, sweaty guys, drugs, alcohol, and false pretenses.

I left the club and walked back to my hotel by myself. The sun was coming up and my friends would be out for several more hours. I just couldn't shake the empty feeling.

As cavalier as I had become about toting stacks of bills in my purse, there were times when the amounts of money I had to ferry around town were way more than fifty grand, and at those times, I took security measures.

I had one driver who I employed specifically for those times.

I arranged to have Silas pick me up because I needed to go downtown to pick up some big money. Silas treated the New York City streets like the setting of his own personal video game, and he could get me from my apartment on the Upper West Side to the Financial District in less than ten minutes.

I stepped into the blacked-out Escalade and pulled out my computer.

"Hi, Molly," Silas said.

"Hey," I said, looking at my spreadsheets.

"How's it going?"

"Fine," I said, distracted by the extreme disparity of what was owed to me versus what I owed. My exposure was enormous and the anxiety of collecting my own money every week was getting to me. Silas wasn't usually this talkative, which was part of why I liked him. I never told him what I did for a living, and although I was sure he knew, he never asked.

"Hey," Silas continued, his Italian accent turning the words into a puddle of sound that I had to wade through to really understand him. "I have some friends who live in Jersey. They run big hedge-fund games . . . they want to meet you."

I looked up from my laptop. The most important part of this job was feeding the game new blood, and while it felt a bit intrusive for Silas to try to get involved, useful tips had come from weirder places.

"Okay," I said. "Give your friend my number, Silas. Thank you."

I smiled at him in the rearview and put my headphones on so I could finish my number crunching uninterrupted for the next six minutes of the ride.

I forgot all about the conversation with Silas until he called me about it, a few hours later.

"I spoke to my friends and they want to meet," he said in his thick accent.

It wasn't strange to me that Silas was acting as a middleman. Everybody always wanted a piece, and if he brokered the deal, he would get one.

"Your friends can meet me at the Four Seasons," I told him. "I'll be there on Friday."

I had already set a meeting there with an art dealer who wanted to start a small weekly game for some dealers, artists, and gallery owners, so this wouldn't waste too much of my time if it turned out to be nothing.

I WAS SITTING IN THE CORNER finishing my iced tea when Silas's "friends" showed up. I noticed them right away. They were two huge men, standing in the bar area, glancing around in confusion. They looked like they had just walked off the set of *Goodfellas*, complete with the shiny suits and the gold chains.

My eyes widened. This was definitely not what I expected and not a meeting I ever wanted to take. However, they had spotted me and were ambling toward me. I stood up to greet them, and they towered over me.

"Uh, are you Molly?" one said, looking confused. I was used to this. Most new players were surprised when I turned out to be a young, petite woman, dressed professionally in an Armani suit and pearls.

"Hi," I said politely, as if nothing was amiss. I motioned to the waiter, who gave my companions a very haughty once-over.

"What would you like to drink?" I asked.

They sat down in the sleek leather chairs, their body language revealing that they felt as out of place as they looked.

"Ah, yeah . . . I'll have, uh . . . apple martini," said the bigger one, who had introduced himself as Nicky. I almost spit my iced tea across the table. The tough guy wanted an apple martini? Really? The whole thing made me want to laugh. The costumes, the fruity girl drink. It was all too much.

The smaller one, Vinny, spoke to me.

"We want to talk about a partnership," he said, his tone letting me know it was more of an order than an offer. "We can help you collect. Nobody will fuck with you. We hear you run a real good game, a nice game, but everyone tries to fuck with you because you're a girl. If you are with us, no one will fuck with you, ever."

As true as his statement was, and as nice an offer as it seemed, I knew it was not on the up-and-up.

I paused and took an extra-long sip of my iced tea.

"Guys, I really appreciate the offer, but I don't really need any help," I said, and tried to make firm but friendly eye contact.

"Look, this ain't Beverly Hills," said Vinny. "This is how it works: you give us a piece and we keep you safe. It's not really an offer, it's just how it is."

"It's just not that kind of game," I said, trying to reason with them. "If I get into bed with you guys, I lose my clients." That was true. It was the absence of a connection to the underworld that kept me in the clear. The cops didn't really care about poker games until they were related to violence, drugs, prostitution, loan sharking. Getting involved with these guys wouldn't keep me safe at all—it would open me up to bigger trouble.

We went back and forth for a bit, talking in circles. Vinny was getting a little heated and Nicky shot him a look.

"Look, let me think about it." I was already racking my brain for a solution, for a way I could be valuable to them without involving them in my business. "Let's talk in a couple days."

I stood to shake their hands, and they towered over me.

"Hey," I offered, almost as an afterthought. "This seems like a hard way to make a living. You know, I know people. If you want to go in a different direction, I could help you, introduce you to some people who could appreciate the unique, uh, skill set you've acquired."

I gave them my most sincere smile and they stared at me like I was from outer space.

"We'll be in touch," said Vinny in a low voice.

NICKY CALLED ME LATER IN THE WEEK.

"Do you really think you could help me?" His voice sounded plaintive, not at all like a posturing tough guy.

"What do you need?"

"I want to do something different. I don't know what, just different."

I silently cheered.

"Sure," I said. "Why don't we meet for lunch after the holidays and discuss?"

"Thanks, Molly," he said.

Thank God, I thought. Problem solved. No need to think about it again.

I barely had time to notice that I had a missed call from Nicky. He called again but I was too inundated with work to respond. I didn't return his next call, or the next. I had bigger problems to deal with: one of my players had written a check for $250,000 that had bounced. And Kenneth was slow paying me the half-million even though he was worth a bajillion.

Then it was Christmas and it was time to go home. I had to. I hadn't been back to Colorado in ages, and I missed my family.

Chapter 30

Colorado was beautiful, covered with pristine white snow. It had been so long since I had been home. I came downstairs in the morning and my mom, grandma, and brothers were sitting around in their pajamas watching a YouTube video of a recent "wish" my brother had granted through his charity, which helped lonely or poor senior citizens realize their lifelong dreams. I took a walk with my mother, and all of the neighbors greeted me by name as we passed. When we visited the local Starbucks, the barista asked me how my day was going, and continued on, asking me what I would do with the remainder of "this beautiful" day. It was so different from my life in New York; it felt like a different planet.

My family was so wonderful, but they were strangers these days. No matter how much older and more accomplished I became, the feeling of inferiority and being an outsider never left. My brothers were both doing remarkable things. Jordan had been accepted into the residency program at Harvard; he married the love of his life and planned to start a family. Jeremy wasted no time after retiring from his illustrious sports career—he immediately launched a tech company and was honored as one of the "30 under 30 in Tech" by *Forbes*. Not only was Jeremy's philanthropy undeniably touching, he received a sizable investment to fund his work and was garnering a lot of good press. I tried to put my feelings of inadequacy aside and simply enjoy and appreciate my family. It was not easy.

At dinner, I stared at my plate, listening to my brothers talk about their lives. Poker was the one thing I was really, really good at. I had built this multimillion-dollar enterprise from scratch, but I still didn't feel like I had a place at the table. I ate quietly, refilling my wineglass too many times. I had nothing worthy to add to the conversation. My family knew about the game. They tried to ignore it, treating it like it was a phase I was going through. A point came when I could no longer control the frustration I felt at being, as I saw it, undervalued; I wanted to rebel. I started talking— about the money, the celebrity and billionaire "friends," the private jets, the full-time driver, the staff, the clubs. Just because my family members didn't find these things impressive didn't mean the rest of the world didn't dream about the life I was describing. I knew I sounded obnoxious.

I could see their eyes judging me, disapproving.

"Is this really the life you want?" asked Jordan.

"Yeah, it is. I don't judge your perfect little rule-following, earnest, boring lives." I was getting angrier, louder, and definitely too drunk.

"I don't give a fuck what you think about my career. You have no idea what I have built, the obstacles I have overcome, so save your self-righteous comments and disapproving looks."

I ran upstairs to my old room, slammed my door, and cried into my pillow. I angrily wiped my eyes and picked up my computer. I was mad at myself and embarrassed; I wanted to leave. I booked a flight and ordered a pickup from a car service.

My mom knocked on the door.

"Honey, we are just worried," she began when she came in. "We love you and we are all so proud of you. You just don't seem like yourself; you seem unhappy."

"There is nothing to worry about, Mom. I'm fine. I'm just tired. I want to lie down, okay?"

"Okay, honey, I love you so much." She hugged me.

I locked the door and packed my bags.

I left a note.

Sorry, just need to get back to NYC.

When the car arrived I walked out of the house with my suitcase. I could hear my family laughing in the living room. I paused for a minute.

They were looking at old photo albums and making fun of each other. I quietly shut the front door behind me. I didn't want to say good-bye; I just wanted to get back to New York as quickly as possible.

ON THE PLANE RIDE BACK TO THE CITY, I thought about the game, the business. It was the only thing that made me feel special, the only thing that hadn't broken my heart. There were challenges, but I always found a way to tackle them. It wasn't just the game; there was a world of opportunities built into it.

The game was my entry into any world I wanted to be a part of. The hedge-fund world. The art world. I could do a game with politicians, artists, royalty. Every subset of every society had gamblers within it, and unearthing them was my specialty.

I meditated on the possibilities during the ride into the city from the airport. New York was covered in snow and festive decorations, and I felt excited to be back. I really did love the city. I felt renewed energy and passion.

I greeted my doorman, Roger, like an old friend and went upstairs.

The building was undergoing construction, and the hallway was empty and quiet. The few tenants who lived there were away for the holidays. Lucy was staying with my neighbor June, who was also her dog walker. I was so excited to see her that I stopped by June's apartment to pick her up. June didn't answer, so I headed upstairs.

Roger knocked on the door with my luggage, more bags than usual because I had brought some things back with me from Colorado.

"Happy holidays, Roger," I said, and tipped him extra-generously.

As he was leaving, I remembered to ask about the mail.

"Were there any packages?"

"I don't think so," he said. "If there are, I'll bring them up."

I thanked him.

I started unpacking when I heard a knock. Probably Roger with my mail, I thought. I opened the door to a stranger. He stepped forward forcefully into the entryway. Before I could protest, he pushed me back and came into my apartment, shutting the door swiftly behind him.

I opened my mouth to scream and he pulled out a gun from under his jacket and slammed me back against the wall. I felt pain radiate down from the center of my skull.

He stuck the barrel of the gun in my mouth.

"Keep your fucking mouth shut," he said. Time slowed down.

A gun in my mouth, there was a gun in my mouth. My teeth chattered as the unforgiving cold steel tapped against them.

Cold fear and adrenaline surged through my veins. I nodded my head to show I would comply and he pulled the revolver out of my mouth and pressed it to the back of my head.

Maybe Roger would come. He was my only hope.

"Walk," he said, moving me with the gun toward my bedroom.

He shoved me in the direction of my bed and I fell forward onto the mattress, exactly where I did not want to be. I was still hoping that Roger would show up, but what if there hadn't been any packages . . . what if he forgot? Or worse, what if this madman shot him?

I needed to pull myself together, but the terror made it so hard to think clearly. I scooted back and sat up against my headboard.

"I have money," I managed to say. "I have a lot of money."

"Where?"

"I have cash in my safe."

He grabbed me by the hair. It still hurt from where he had smashed me against the wall. I felt dizzy.

"Where?"

"In my closet." I motioned to the corner of my room.

Okay, this was good. Maybe he was here for money. A tiny bit of clarity returned. I looked at his face; he had dark hair, large dark eyes. He was cleanly shaven. Why didn't he have a mask on? WHY WASN'T HE WEARING A MASK? As things stood, I could easily identify him . . . The answer hit me like a brick.

He's going to kill me.

I had left my family without saying good-bye. I had been awful and mean.

He's going to kill me.

He grabbed my arm and led me to the closet, then put his hand on my shoulder and shoved me onto my knees. My body had gone limp, the realization that these were most likely my last few minutes on this earth had replaced the fear with grief.

He gestured toward the safe with the gun.

Numbly I entered my code into the keypad. The gun was pressing against my skull.

The metal door swung open to reveal the neatly organized, rubber-banded stacks of $10,000 and jewelry boxes within, along with important documents like my birth certificate and passport.

"Give me the cash and the jewelry," he said. I could detect excitement in his voice.

I passed him the stacks.

I handed him the jewelry my grandmother had left me.

"Give me a bag," he ordered. He would need it to carry all the cash. I stood up carefully and handed him a Balmain bag from my extensive collection of designer purses.

He shoved the stacks, a gold locket with a picture of my great-grandmother who was my namesake, my mother's wedding ring, and a pair of diamond earrings from my grandmother inside. He zipped the bag closed looking very pleased.

Then he stooped down to where I was kneeling and grabbed my face with his rough and callused hands, shoving his face up against mine. His breath smelled like tooth decay and cigarettes.

He pressed his mouth against my ear and whispered, "You still think you can call the shots, you little fucking cunt?"

"What do you mean?" I asked weakly

"This is your fault. If you weren't such a bitch to my friends, I wouldn't have to do what I have to do."

And that was the moment when it made sense: he had been sent by the guys I met at the Four Seasons.

He ran the back of his hand down my cheek.

"It's such a shame, you have such a pretty face."

He pulled me to my feet by my hair.

He slammed my head into the wall. Everything was spinning. I was crying. As soon as I opened my eyes again, I felt his fist connect with my cheek. He hit me again in the nose.

It felt like all my nerves exploded, then numbness. My hand flew to my face; blood was gushing out of my nose and into my mouth. I couldn't breathe. I was choking on my own blood. He hit me again. His fist felt like an iron bar as it slammed against the delicate bones of my face. I imagined all of the bones breaking, splintering into little pieces. My face felt like it was blowing up like a balloon. I cried out and tried to get away from him, but there was nowhere to go in the closet, and I pushed myself back as far as I could, pressed against the dresses and coats, bleeding on rustling silk and smooth, soft fur.

Everything hurt. It hurt so much it almost stopped hurting, like it was one complete feeling that just changed the way it felt to be alive. I was like an animal, gasping, trapped.

He pulled me out of the closet and then took his gun out of his jacket.

I saw my mom and dad's faces, my brothers, Lucy, Eugene.

"Please, I have a family. Please don't kill me," I choked. I didn't care what he wanted, I would do anything. I just didn't want to die.

"Molly," he said, and now his voice was as gentle as his hand on my back, and sad. "I told you. We didn't want it to be like this . . ."

He pointed the gun at my face. I winced and shut my eyes. It felt like an eternity.

"Open your eyes. We could have a very good relationship, just don't disrespect us ever again."

I managed to nod my head.

"And don't even think about calling the police. We know where your mom lives—a real pretty house in the Colorado mountains."

Oh God, oh God, what have I done?

"I won't . . . I promise," I sobbed

"This is your one and only warning."

I saw his fist come at me again, and then, blackness.

When I came to I was alone. My whole body felt limp and I crawled toward the front door, lifted myself up by the handle, and closed the dead bolt. Then I sat with my back against the door, waiting, listening.

I couldn't call anyone, not the police, not building security, not a boyfriend or my friends. Maybe I could call Eugene.

I dialed his number.

"What's up?" he asked. He had been cold and distant ever since I'd begun dating Glen.

"Eugene, can you come over? I need you." My voice was weak and tearful.

"Oh, now that you aren't with Glen you need me? Sorry, Zil, you made your decision. I'm busy."

"Please, Eug," I begged

"I can't, I'm sorry." And he hung up.

I was completely alone.

I don't know how long I sat with my back to the door. I felt weak and frozen. When I finally got up on shaky legs and went into the bathroom, my reflection in the mirror was horrific. My eyes were swollen and black, my lip was cut and bloody, and there was dried blood caked all over my face, neck, and chest. My clothes were covered in blood. It was like looking at someone else's image. I got in the shower and stood under the water, the heat of it blasting my bruised and cut skin. I didn't care. I sank to my knees and sobbed under the water, crying for the things I had lost, for the loneliness, for all the things I had hoped I would be.

Most of all, I sobbed because I knew I wasn't going to walk away—even now, even after this.

Chapter 31

I spent New Year's Eve by myself, waiting for my bruises to heal. I lied to my friends, I lied to my parents. I stared numbly out of my window as midnight struck and 2011 arrived. I didn't leave my apartment for a week. I spent most of the time in bed, curled up with Lucy, who looked at me with her deep, soulful, concerned eyes. When I finally went out, I thought I saw my attacker's face everywhere. I was sure my driver had been in on it, almost positive one of the doormen had taken cash to give him entry. I trusted no one.

I got another call from Vinny. This time I called him back.

"Molly, how are you?"

"Fine," I said.

"Let's have another meeting. I think you will see things clearer now."

"Okay," I said.

I didn't have a choice and I knew it.

"Next week," I said. "I'm traveling this week." I couldn't face him with the bruises. I wouldn't give him the satisfaction.

The day before I was supposed to meet with the men responsible for having me beaten and robbed, the men who I might be forced to make some sort of deal with, I picked up the *New York Times*. On the front page I saw:

NEARLY 125 ARE ARRESTED IN SWEEPING FBI MOB ROUNDUP

I read on. This was the biggest mob takedown in New York City history.

I never got the call I was expecting from Vinny . . . or anyone else. I couldn't believe how lucky I was.

MY LUCK DIDN'T LAST FOR LONG: A subpoena arrived via certified mail. Brad Ruderman, one of my players from my old L.A. game had been indicted by the federal government. Allegedly his fund had been a Ponzi scheme. "Bad Brad" Ruderman was known in my games in Los Angeles as "free money." It became routine after I sent out the invitation text for the weekly game that everyone responded with, "Is Brad playing?" He was so bad it often felt like he was trying to lose. No one could actually play the cards that poorly after two years of steady practice. And then there was Brad.

I knew him well, so after he'd been in my game for a couple months, I had pulled him aside.

"This may not be for you," I said, gently, and offered him poker lessons. I wanted Brad to play, but I wanted him to have a chance to win.

Even Tobey tried to help him learn how to play, which shocked me a bit until I understood what his motivation must have been: Tobey loved the game when Brad was in it because it attracted the "A-team" players. Brad needed to get better so he would keep coming back. If he lost too much, he'd quit.

I liked him, but there was always something strange, something off with Brad. To me, he seemed a bit lost. We became friendly enough that when his mother passed, I went to the funeral. He seemed a bit tortured too, but he was generally very nice. Now I understood why his affect had been so odd: he had been hiding a giant secret. Most of the investors in Brad's fund were family and friends. He wasn't even registered with the SEC, and at the time of his arrest he had only $60,000 in his fund—a far cry from the $45 million he reported to his investors. That's why, even though he never won, he kept playing. Suddenly it all made sense. He may have lost $5.3 million in the game, but he had used the playing field to raise millions, getting the other guys to invest with him as he allowed them to take his money.

Now the prosecutor wanted my deposition. Brad had already disclosed information about the game, the players, the amount he lost, who the checks went to, and allegedly that the game was run and orchestrated by me. I kept reading the subpoena. Brad was claiming that I lured him into my games and that in these clandestine rooms he had developed a gambling addiction which led him to lose sight of his morals, culminating in the Ponzi scheme.

So I flew to Los Angeles.

MY OLD, L.A. ATTORNEY picked me up at the airport. The deposition was as unpleasant as I had expected. After hours of skirting questions and only confirming innocuous details, I was exhausted. The questions dredged up memories of my L.A. life, which I had pushed into that corner of my mind that I refused to visit.

It had been so long since I was back in California. I was staying at the Four Seasons; the hotel held so many memories for me, and it felt like there were many ghosts haunting the halls, but so much had changed. I was a different person. And the L.A. game had changed too. Rick Salomon had accused Arthur Grossman of cheating, and even though he recanted his accusation, he was no longer invited. Most interesting of all, Tobey was rarely invited anymore either.

Arthur had become the biggest winner in the game, allowing one of the local pros to play in exchange for lessons. The dealers were on salary and the girls came and went based on their current girlfriend status.

I sat on my patio looking out on the city I felt I had once presided over. The familiar landmarks, the view that used to invoke such a feeling of confidence and triumph, now seemed to shun me.

I wondered if, in the end, Tobey felt like it had all been worth it.

Chapter 32

*I*t was early March and once again the cold winter was giving way to more temperate weather, raising my spirits along with it. I was racing around the city, taking meetings, making deals, and unearthing new gamblers in New York. My visit to Los Angeles had reminded me that I had lost everything and rebuilt once before, and that I could do it again. So that was my current plan: to rebuild my empire in New York—but not forever. When I was ready, I would exit gracefully and start a new life as far from poker as possible.

I was on my own now, distrustful and wary of bringing anyone close, but that was safe. And I was discovering the charm of a new breed of clientele: wealthy Russians. I was intrigued by this new subset of players. They possessed both hardness and a kind of generosity, and they respected me, even revered me.

They also loved luxury, they appreciated the details, and they seemed to have very little attachment to money—they seemed to acquire it effortlessly and part with it with the same ease. It was one of several nuances in this community's behavioral style that I found fascinating, like the way they never asked one another what their business was. Such a line of inquiry would have been considered rude. What had been the most common question among my American players—"So what do you do, bro?"—would have netted you disdain and disrespect with my new Russian friends.

I became particularly close with a man named Alex, who seemed to be a leader of sorts. He was incredibly intelligent, sophisticated and mysterious, with a quiet but stately composure.

In New York there seemed to be a never-ending supply of Russians with fancy cars, fancy shoes, and fancy watches who wanted to play. They all seemed to have bottomless pockets. They didn't complain, they paid promptly, they didn't ask for deals, and they wanted to play every day of the week.

I was back on my way up, and I liked the international flavor.

I HAD ALSO REBUILT MY BIG GAME, and it was better than ever. Along with the Russians, the Wall Street guys, the athletes, and the celebrities were back. I had an epic game planned for this evening—one of my huge London players was in town, and the Russians said they were bringing some guys visiting from Moscow who were allegedly some of the biggest gamblers in the world. If the night went as planned, it would serve as solid proof that I could always come back, better, stronger—no matter who tried to knock me down.

I was at my vanity preparing for the game. It was 10 P.M. and I had just returned from a collection run that had taken much longer than I'd anticipated.

I quickly applied my makeup, and then my phone rang. It was a blocked number.

"Yes?" I said, looking in the mirror.

"Don't go to your game tonight," a muffled voice warned.

"Who is this?" I demanded.

The line went dead.

Since the attack at my apartment, I had begun to change the venues of my games regularly and had hired security guards.

I was on top again. I figured that the voice on the phone belonged to one of my competitors, and that he was trying to scare me.

I finished dressing, trying to ignore the cryptic call. I slid on a white silk dress, nude, strappy stilettos, my silver fox coat, and a vintage Dior diamond bracelet. The Russians made it fun to dress up again; they were appreciative of glamour and presentation. I gave myself one last glance in the mirror and headed out. I called for the elevator. Then my phone started buzzing incessantly. I fished it out and glanced at the message.

I looked down at the text message from Peter, a player who was already at the game. I was standing in the elevator bank. The elevator arrived, the doors slid open, and I let them close, just standing there in shock.

The FBI is here!! 20 or so. They are looking for you.

I read the words over and over, trying to make some sense.

I stood still. Everything else kept moving forward. The whole universe was spinning and I was frozen in that hallway. After a moment the trance lifted. The elevator came and went, the doors opened and closed, and I reacted. I rushed back into my apartment.

I felt I had very little time to act. The agents must have realized by now that I wasn't at the game. My apartment would be their next stop, if they were not already at the entrance to the building, poised and waiting for me to step out. *The feds. THE FEDS.*

This was infinitely bigger than anything I had ever anticipated. I was terrified. I wanted my mom. I grabbed my purse, a hastily packed suitcase, and Lucy and bolted out the door.

I closed my eyes, hoping the FBI wouldn't be waiting in my lobby as we rode down the twenty-one floors. The door opened, I braced myself.

Nobody was there.

We walked to the front doors and pushed through into the cool night air. I held my breath as we stepped onto the curb, waiting for lights and yells and panic. There was nothing unusual, just passersby dressed in business casual and the stink of the carriage horses from across the street in Central Park.

My black Escalade was waiting

I turned around and looked at my glamorous dream apartment. The EMPIRE sign on the side of the building glowed in red letters. I felt sad. Somehow I knew it was the last time I would ever be here.

"WHERE TO?" SAID MY NEW DRIVER, Joe, jovial and relaxed.

It struck me that not everybody's world was ending tonight. Just mine.

"Joe," I said. "We've got to get out of here. Please. Quickly."

"Where to, Miss Bloom?"

"Just drive, please," I said.

I called my attorney at home

"I'm sorry to disturb you. The feds raided my game tonight. They broke down the door and they were looking for me."

"Where are you?" he asked, going from sleeping to sharp and alert in one second.

"I'm in a car, headed to the airport. I want to go home, to Colorado." My voice cracked. "Is—is it a crime to leave the state?"

I couldn't believe the words that were coming out of my mouth.

"No, it's not a crime, but they may very well be at the airport to apprehend you. Just stay in New York tonight. Check into a hotel, stay at a friend's, and I'll deal with this first thing in the morning."

"I really just want to go home. I'll call you from Colorado."

"If they arrest you, don't say anything. Call me and I'll come down. *Remember, do not say anything.*"

"Okay," I answered.

I booked a flight out of Newark airport on my credit card.

Then I told my driver to drop me off at JFK.

If the feds were tracking me, I hoped this would throw them off. Every second felt like an eternity. I walked up to the ticketing desk. I stared nervously at the face of the airline agent as she entered my information into the system.

My flight didn't leave for a couple hours, so I took Lucy and my suitcase and I locked myself in a stall in one of the bathrooms. We sat and waited for hours.

Finally it was time to board the plane. I approached my gate. This was it. If I made it past here, I would be home, at least for a moment, at least long enough to see my parents and hug them good-bye.

The sun was coming up over New York City. I watched the island fade as a new day started and the plane ascended into the clouds. I wanted to cry, but I felt numb and dead inside. When we landed I got my bags and found my driver.

He took the familiar route to my family home in the mountains, memories of my childhood skiing every weekend with my family playing out in my head.

Finally we pulled into the driveway at my mom's house. I rang the door-bell, and she answered in her robe. Her eyes flew open in surprise when she saw me. I fell into her, going limp.

"Honey, what's wrong?" she said."Tell me, honey, you can tell me, are you all right?"

And then I collapsed in tears. My mom held me and I couldn't stop sobbing.

AFTER I TOLD MY MOM what had happened, I crawled into her bed and she stayed with me, stroking my head until I fell into a dreamless sleep. I woke up as the sun was setting. Nestled there in the woods, I felt worlds away from my poker life. I felt like I could just hide in this house forever. But I knew I couldn't, I had to face this.

I called my attorney; he said I was part of an investigation, and this would require an extra fee for him to work on my behalf. I logged into my bank account.

My balance read: –9,999,999.00. I checked my other accounts, and they reflected the same negative balance.

I called my bank,

"I need to know why all my accounts have a negative balance."

"I'm sorry, Miss Bloom," the bank officer I was speaking with said awkwardly. "There is a note here to contact the United States District Attorney's office."

I immediately called my lawyer, who informed me that my assets had been seized by the government. He informed me that the government wanted me to come in and "talk to them" about organized crime.

I thought about the soulless eyes of my attacker in New York, and especially about his threat against my mother.

"No, I won't to do that," I said firmly.

"I'll let them know," he said.

"What happens now?" I asked

"Well, if you don't cooperate, I can't get your money back and there is a possibility they could indict you."

"But we analyzed the laws," I said, referring to the research I'd had him do on the federal statutes around poker. His professional opinion, as well as my L.A. attorney's, had been that I was not violating federal law—so the fact that I could be federally indicted was mind-boggling.

"The government does this sometimes, they try to squeeze people for information," my attorney informed me.

I had no money, no answers, and no desire to go into a witness protection program.

I had arrived in New York just a few years prior in a flash and a fury, and I left in silence and alone.

My phone stopped ringing, the girls went away. I sold my poker table and Shuffle Master, I gave up my apartment. I paid movers to pack a life into boxes and store it somewhere in Queens.

I MOVED HOME. I tried to learn how to live quietly, in nature. There were so many unanswered questions. The fear of the unknown was a constant underlying presence in my life. I had good days and bad days. Sometimes I felt an incredible sense of relief and sometimes I was so depressed I couldn't get out of my bed.

I remembered an old pro I had met in the poker room at the Bellagio. At the time I was trying to land a huge whale and I was keeping my eye on him while pretending to watch Eugene play.

He sat to my left; he had just gotten a bad beat. He turned to me with wise eyes and announced, "Poker will break your heart, young lady."

"Oh," I said, smiling. "I don't play."

"We all play," he replied. "Poker is the game of life."

He was right. Poker had broken my heart.

I learned to live through it, though. I went for hikes, I read, and I wrote.

My brother and I went for a seven-day trek through Peru, ending at Machu Picchu. There, I sat atop a hill and marveled at the astounding masterpiece around me—the legacy that this great civilization had left behind. I thought about the game. When I was holding court in those decadent penthouses, I felt like I was at the top of the world, but it was a material world. There was so much excitement and drama around me. All the kings of that world sat together, playing with their empires. When the last card was dealt, when the table was put away, after the maids came through, there was no evidence of the rivalries, no vestiges of glory, no great monuments to victory. There was just silence, as if it had never happened at all.

Epilogue

spent two years putting the pieces of my life back together. Six months after the feds raided my game, they arrested Alex, and a few of the other Russians. They allegedly were running a huge scam, they had defrauded the insurance companies out of $600 million. My attorney said that was almost certainly why the feds had gotten involved. I knew that the powerful network I had spent years building and the relationships I had cultivated were no longer viable. Not only had word spread within the poker community, but there had been a lot of press stemming from the Bradley Ruderman indictment and a subsequent lawsuit in which every player who took a check from Brad in the poker game was getting sued. Many of those players were celebrities, and with a little digging, reporters exposed the games, the players, and the girl who ran the whole operation. They called me the "Poker Princess," the "Madam of Poker," and worse. Paparazzi came to my mother's house, my father's house, my high school. They called my friends, my ex-boyfriends, and e-mailed me incessantly. I spoke to no one, and finally they just went away.

I moved back to L.A. right before my birthday, almost two years to the day after my world fell apart. I found a cute apartment, nothing like the luxurious homes I had in my previous life, but I made it my own. Most of my "friends" had jumped ship when the money was gone, but I was left with the few quality friends I had made along the way and I was grateful for them. I was walking Lucy early one morning and I ran smack into Eugene. There he was, as if no time had passed, with his dark eyes smiling at me. He had moved to Los Angeles and by chance was renting an apartment a couple of blocks from mine.

"Zilla!" he said in his soft voice, and hugged me tightly.

I was so happy he had gotten out of New York. Last I'd heard he was partnering with Eddie Ting, who had, predictably, screwed him over. We talked for a long time, reminisced about our good times, crazy times. I apologized for the way I had treated him.

"I'll always love you, Zil," he said, "and I forgave you a long time ago. You are the strongest, prettiest girl I know, with the smallest feet and little wings."

I laughed. I missed him so much, missed living in our fantasy world. He was the only person who really knew me, really saw me, and vice versa. He was my soul mate, and the way I felt about him was visceral, but I knew we could never be a couple. He was a gambler; he would always live at night, live for the next hand, the next game, the next move. We looked at each other; all the passion, love, and history was dizzying.

"I better go," I said, somewhat reluctantly.

"Okay," he said.

We hugged good-bye.

I walked home thinking about the irony that he had moved so close. I thought about my crazy life in poker, and I missed it sometimes. The danger, the money, the excitement, but it wasn't sustainable. I had learned to live differently now. I slept a lot, spent time outside in the sun, I ate healthy meals, I lived frugally. It was peaceful.

WHEN I GOT READY FOR BED THAT NIGHT, I put on the silky, white La Perla nightgown that Eugene had given me on my birthday long ago.

I smiled. He was doing well and that was all I ever wanted for him. I wrote a little before dozing off to sleep, cuddling with Lucy, the one true constant in my life.

I woke to my phone ringing incessantly. Confused, I looked at the time. Five A.M.? I didn't get calls from strange numbers at strange hours anymore. I answered.

"Molly Bloom?"

"Yes?"

"This is Jeremy Wesson from the FBI. We are outside your apartment. If you don't come our immediately, we will break down the door. You have twenty seconds."

I bolted up, my heart racing and my hands shaking. Was this a prank, was someone trying to hurt me? I didn't understand.

"You have fifteen seconds, Miss Bloom."

I ran to the door and opened it.

It was a scene out of a movie, FBI agents, maybe twenty of them, maybe more. Assault weapons, handcuffs, voices screaming at me, the things they yell at violent criminals. They only took off my handcuffs to let me put on different clothes. I had to change in front of the female agents. No underwire bra, they commanded. They wouldn't let me touch anything, so they dressed me. After placing the handcuffs on again, they put me in a dark SUV.

"Where are we going?" I asked quietly.

"Downtown," was all they would say.

We pulled into a dark basement parking garage.

"Are you ready for the prisoner?" a man asked into a two-way radio.

"Yes," they answered.

They led me upstairs, and announced something about the prisoner being on the floor.

They took my fingerprints, my picture, and then they asked me to stand and face the wall. A female agent put shackles on my feet.

"Turn around," she commanded.

She took a large chain belt and fastened it around my waist. She then handcuffed my hands to the chain belt and she and another agent led me to a cell. It was hard to walk with the shackles, they were cutting into my anklebone, but I didn't dare complain. They opened the door to a dirty cell. I looked at their faces, terrified. They led me inside and with a large key they locked me in.

"How long will I be here?" I asked politely

"I would get comfortable, sweetheart," the woman said.

I heard the marshals call out, "Prisoners on the floor!" My head snapped up. I waited as the shuffle of feet rounded the corner. My eyes connected with familiar dark almond eyes . . . *Eugene!* I searched his face and he looked at me for a moment and then turned away coldly. Behind him was his brother, Illya; Helly, the wealthy socialite; Noah, the mathematician called "the oracle," who served as the group's sports handicapper; and then came Bryan Zuriff, a trust-fund kid. When my lawyer finally showed up, he handed me the thick indictment, which detailed the alleged criminal conspiracy. It read like a movie script. The defendants ranged from a man known as a "Vor," a Russian organized-crime boss who was also one of the ten most wanted fugitives in the world; to Helly, the wealthy playboy who had dated a countless number of supermodels; to John Hansen, the chess master; to Noah, the math savant; to Pete the Plumber, who had lost so much gambling that he had given away part of his plumbing business, now allegedly being used as a front for money laundering. And then there was Eugene, his brother, and their father, who according to the indictment were running a $100-million bookmaking operation out of the Trump Tower apartment where I had spent many nights.

There were thirty-four defendants, most I had never heard of.

I was the only woman.

Finally I was released on $100,000 bail and ordered to appear in New York City before the federal judge of the southern district of the city to enter a plea.

BEING IN THE COURTROOM WAS one of the most bizarre experiences of my life. On the benches on the left side of the courtroom sat friends, family, and reporters. I glanced at my mom, who, unbeknownst to her, was sitting next to Eugene's mother, who looked distraught. My heart broke for this woman; her whole family had been indicted. The benches on the right side of the room were for defendants, and the ones who were still incarcerated sat behind a glass partition at the head of the courtroom. My lawyers sat reassuringly on either side of me, explaining everything that was happening and making sure I was doing okay. I looked around at my so-called coconspirators. Some were in slick suits, some in matching velour tracksuits, and some in prison uniforms. I had read the press release on the FBI website. I was facing five to ten years.

The judge entered and we all rose. Most of the speech he made was about procedure. I looked around for Eugene; he was sitting in the front row, dressed casually. I waited as each defendant, many needing translators, entered in pleas of not guilty. Finally, at the very end of the list, he called my name. I stood, although I could barely feel my legs. The whole courtroom turned and looked at me and I felt the room start to spin.

"How do you plead, Miss Bloom?"

"Not guilty, Your Honor," I managed.

"I'm sorry. I couldn't hear you all the way back there. How do you plead to the charges alleged against you?"

The whole courtroom was still. Somehow I tapped into an extra reserve of strength I didn't know I had.

I spoke in a loud strong voice: "I plead not guilty to the charges, Your Honor."

The year of my life following my arrest and indictment was heartbreaking and terrifying, but it was also a year of tremendous growth. I decided not to fight the indictment. Unfortunately, it is not always a case of guilt or innocence. If I had chosen to fight, it would have cost me millions of dollars (I barely had enough money to travel to the mandated court dates) as well as years of my life—all with no guarantee of justice. I also declined once more to cooperate with the government. So, on the coldest day of the year, December 12, 2013, I threw down the white flag and accepted the charges. I became a convicted felon that day, and I await sentencing.

I don't know how the honorable federal judge will sentence me, but I know that no matter what he decrees, he doesn't decide my fate. *I* do. I have been asked many times: If I had to do it all over, would I choose the same path? My answer is yes, a thousand times, yes. I had a grand adventure. I learned to believe in myself. I was brave, and I went big. I was also reckless and selfish. I got lost along the way. I abandoned the things that mattered and traded them for wealth and statues. I lusted for power and I hurt people. But I was forced to face myself, to lose everything, to fall on my face in front of the world, and the lessons I learned on the way up were just as valuable as the ones on the way down. I know that this time I will use everything I have learned to do something that matters.

Acknowledgments

Writing this book has not been without its challenges. I want to acknowledge those who stood by my side, encouraged, and believed in me.

Carrie, thank you for believing in my story and for working tirelessly to make the book what it is. You have been an extraordinary collaborator and friend.

Lisa Gallagher, I feel like I met you a million lifetimes ago. We have been through so much together. You have gone above and beyond, both as a friend and an agent. I can't imagine a more brilliant, savvy, and compassionate partner to have gone on this journey with.

Susan, you are amazing. Your hard work and kindness were an integral part of this process.

Lynn, my publisher, thank you for all your support.

Joseph, thank you for your creativity and vision.

Matthew, I am so grateful for our serendipitous meeting several years ago. You have become one of my closest friends and most trusted advisors. I am a big fan of the Hiltzik clan. Thank you for your help and guidance and for always making me laugh.

Jim Walden, how can I possibly thank you enough? You are a true gladiator. Your integrity, compassion, and unwavering commitment to justice restored my hope in my darkest hour.

Sarah Vacchiano, your kindness and competence have meant more than you will ever know. I am honored to have you on my side and as my friend.

Leopoldo, what can I say, you have been such an integral part of both the book and my entire life. You light up the world with your radiant goodness. I love you so much.

Jordan and Jeremy, thank you for your unconditional love. I am astounded more and more each day at what extraordinary human beings you have become. You are not only my brothers but my best friends.

Gram, I feel blessed to have spent so much time with you, both as a child and then again as an adult. I love you.

Ali, I feel overwhelmed and filled with love just writing your name. You have stood by me with no hesitation, no judgments. You nursed my broken spirit with both kindness and gentle guidance. You taught me by example the value of gratitude, compassion, and generosity. You are my best friend, my sister, and my compass. There are no words to describe my gratitude adequately—just a lifetime of trying to be as good to you as you are to me and the rest of the world. You truly are my hero.

Steph, you are such a huge inspiration to me. Thanks for the unconditional friendship, the strategy sessions, and for your unwavering support.

LL, you were one of the first friends I made in L.A. Thanks for coming back into my life when I needed you most.

And finally, Dad, you have always been larger than life to me. You taught me to be fearless and to believe in my dreams, and you gave me the encouragement and mentoring to achieve them.

I love you, Daddy.